愛 ❤ 英閱

擁抱英語文選＼深度閱讀合輯

Michaeline Wu／Bai Yang 著

Dennis Le Boeuf／Liming Jing 審訂

CONTENTS Part 1 Reading Inspiration

I ESSAYS & PROSE

2 SPEECHES & SAYINGS

3 **BIOGRAPHIES & DIARIES**

CONTENTS Part 1 Reading Inspiration

4　STORIES & FABLES

CONTENTS Part 2 Reading Moments

CONTENTS Part 2 Reading Moments

CONTENTS Part 2 Reading Moments

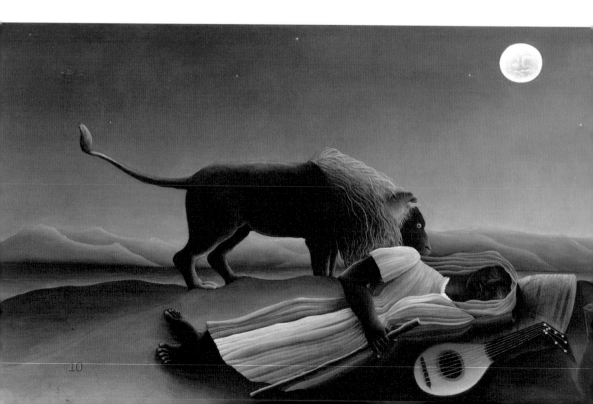

Part 1__
Reading Inspiration

1 Essays & Prose

Reading

🎧 1 It is not all books that are as dull as their readers. There are probably words addressed to our condition exactly, which, if we could really hear and understand, would be more salutary¹ than the morning or the spring to our lives, and possibly put a new aspect on the face of things for us. How many a man has dated a new era in his life from the reading of a book. The book exists for us perchance² which will explain our miracles and reveal new ones. The at-present unutterable³ things we may find somewhere uttered. These same questions that disturb and puzzle⁴ and confound⁵ us have in their turn occurred to all the wise men; not one has been omitted; and each has answered them, according to his ability, by his words and his life.

↗ Henry David Thoreau (1817-1862): *Walden* ✶

Comprehension

🍂 *According to Henry Thoreau, what are the benefits of reading a book?*

🍁 *What can books tell us about the history and the future?*

1. salutary ['sæljʊterɪ] (a.) promoting good health 有益的
2. perchance [pər'tʃæns] (adv.) perhaps; maybe 或許;可能
3. unutterable [ʌn'ʌtərəbəl] (a.) beyond the power of words
   非言語所能形容的
4. puzzle ['pʌzəl] (v.) to confuse somebody by being difficult or impossible to understand 使迷惑
5. confound [kən'faʊnd] (v.) to cause confusion or mix up 使困惑

The library in Palais Dumba (Carl Ritter von Dombrowski, 1872-1951)

2 Library

 Be a little careful about your library. Do you foresee what you will do with it? Very little to be sure. But the real question is, what it will do with you? You will come here and get books that will open your eyes, and your ears, and your curiosity, and turn you inside out or outside in.

↗ Ralph Waldo Emerson (1803-1882): *Journals*

I go into my library, and all history unrolls before me. I breathe the morning air of the world while the scent[1] of Eden's roses yet lingered[2] in it, while it vibrated only to the world's first brood[3] of nightingales[4], and to the laugh of Eve. I see the pyramids building; I hear the shoutings of the armies of Alexander[5].

↗ Alexander Smith (1948-):
Books and Gardens ★

Comprehension

🍂 *According to the passage of Ralph Waldo Emerson, why do you have to be careful about the library?*

🍁 *Why can a library turn our "inside out or outside in"? What does the expression mean here?*

🍃 *What did Alexander Smith learn in the library?*

1. scent [sɛnt] (n.) a distinctive, often agreeable odor or smell 香味；氣味
2. linger ['lɪŋgər] (v.) to be slow in parting, hesitate in leaving 流連
3. brood [bruːd] (n.) a group of young birds all born at the same time 同一窩孵出的幼禽
4. nightingale ['naɪtɪŋgeɪl] (n.) a European songbird (Luscinia megarhynchos) with reddish brown plumage known for its sweet songs of the male at night during the breeding season 夜鶯
5. Alexander: the king of Macedon who conquered Greece, Egypt, and Persia (356-323 BC); also known as Alexander the Great 亞歷山大大帝，馬其頓國王，憑武力征服希臘、埃及與波斯

3 Civilization

🎧 3 🎧 Greek civilization—that it is so interesting. Do not tell me only, say human nature, of the magnitude[1] of your industry and commerce[2]; of the beneficence[3] of your institutions, your freedom, your equality; of the great and growing number of your churches and schools, libraries, and newspapers; tell me also if your civilization—which is the grand name you give to all this development— tell me if your civilization is interesting.

↗ Matthew Arnold (1822-1888):
Civilization in the United States ✶

Comprehension

🍁 *According to Matthew Arnold, what are the elements of a civilization?*

1. magnitude ['mægnɪtuːd] (n.) greatness of size or extent 巨大；廣大
2. commerce ['kɑːmɜːrs] (n.) the buying and selling of things on a large scale, which involves transportation from place to place 商業
3. beneficence [bɪ'nefɪsəns] (n.) the quality of being kind or doing good 慈善；善行

4 Knowledge

🎧 4 Knowledge is happiness, because to have knowledge—broad, deep knowledge—is to know true ends from false, and lofty[1] things from low. To know the thoughts and deeds that have marked man's progress is to feel the great heartthrobs[2] of humanity through the centuries; and if one does not feel in these pulsations[3] a heavenward[4] striving[5], one must indeed be deaf to the harmonies of life.

↗ Helen Keller (1880-1968):
The Story of My Life ⚹

Comprehension

🍁 *What is "knowledge" according to Keller?*

1. lofty [ˈlɔːfti] (a.) exalted and refined 高尚的
2. heartthrob [ˈhɑːrtθrɑːb] (n.) heartbeat, the throb of a heart 心跳
3. pulsation [pʌlˈseɪʃən] (n.) rhythmic beating or vibrating 律動
4. heavenward [ˈhevənwərd] (a.) toward or in the direction of heaven 朝天堂的
5. striving [straɪvɪŋ] (n.) an effortful attempt to attain a goal 努力；奮鬥

5 Learning

5 There are some things which cannot be learned quickly, and time, which is all we have, must be paid heavily for their acquiring[1]. They are the very simplest things and because it takes a man's life to know them, the little new that each man gets from life are very costly and the only heritage[2] he has to leave.

↗ Ernest Hemingway (1899-1961):
Death in the Afternoon ⁎

Comprehension

🍂 *According to the passage, what would be one of the "things" that fits Hemingway's description?*
a. the theory of relativity
b. life experience
c. money
d. school degree

1. acquire [əˈkwaɪr] (v.) to get or obtain possession of something 獲得
2. heritage [ˈherɪtɪdʒ] (n.) something that is passed down by the previous generations 遺產

Spring (Sir Lawrence Alma-Tadema, 1836-1912)

6 Happiness

The great end of all human industry is the attainment[1] of happiness. For this were arts invented, sciences cultivated[2], laws ordained[3], and societies modeled, by the most profound[4] wisdom of patriots[5] and legislators. Even the lonely savage[6], who lies exposed[7] to the inclemency[8] of the elements and the fury[9] of wild beasts, forgets not, for a moment, this grand object of his being.

↗ David Hume (1711-1776) *

Comprehension

🍁 *What did Hume consider to be a common goal for all human beings? Do you value the same goal?*

🍁 *What have people done to achieve this goal?*

🍁 *There is a famous saying that "Hell hath no fury like a woman scorned." Do you know what it means??*

1. attainment [əˈteɪnmənt] (n.) the act of achieving an end 達到；獲得
2. cultivate [ˈkʌltɪveɪt] (v.) to foster the growth of 培育
3. ordain [ɔːrˈdeɪn] (v.) to establish or order by appointment, decree, or law 制訂（法律等）
4. profound [prəˈfaʊnd] (a.) having intellectual depth and insight 深奧的；深遠的
5. patriot [ˈpeɪtriət] (n.) a person who loves his or her country and supports its authority and interests 愛國者
6. savage [ˈsævɪdʒ] (n.) a person belonging to a primitive society, an uncivilized person 野蠻人
7. expose [ɪkˈspoʊz] (v.) to deprive of shelter, protection, or care and be subject to risk from a harmful action or condition 暴露
8. inclemency [ɪnˈklemənsi] (n.) stormy and windy weather 惡劣的天氣
9. fury [ˈfjʊri] (n.) wild and violent anger 暴怒

7 Truth

I would have you a man of sense as well as sensibility[1]. You will find goodness and truth everywhere you go. If you have to choose, choose truth. For that is closest to Earth. Keep close to Earth, my boy: in that lies strength. Simplicity[2] of heart is just as necessary to an architect as for a farmer or a minister if the architect is going to build great buildings.

The Blind Girl (John Everett Millais , 1829-1896)

↗ Anna Wright ✳

Comprehension

🍂 *Why did Wright suggest choosing truth over goodness?*

🍁 *According to the passage, do you think Wright would prefer a community of houses or a tall skyscraper?*

1. sensibility [ˌsensɪˈbɪlɪti] (n.) the capacity for physical sensation, ability to feel 感覺；敏感
2. simplicity [sɪmˈplɪsəti] (n.) the quality of being simple or plain and not complicated or difficult 簡單；單純

8 Science and Art

There are two kinds of truth; the truth that lights the way and the truth that warms the heart. The first of these is science, and the second is art. Without art, science would be as useless as a pair of high forceps[1] in the hands of a plumber. Without science, art would become a crude[2] mess[3] of folklore[4] and emotional quackery[5].

↗ Raymond Chandler (1888-1959):
Great Thought ✴

Comprehension

🍁 *According to Raymond Chandler, what are the two kinds of "truth"?*

🍁 *Which of the two kinds of "truth" is more important to you? Why?*

1. forceps ['fɔːrseps] (n.) an instrument for grasping, holding, or pulling on things especially for delicate operations (as by jewelers or surgeons) 鑷子；鉗子
2. crude [kruːd] (a.) lacking finish, grace, tact, or taste; uncultured 粗糙的；粗陋的
3. mess [mes] (n.) a state of disorder, untidiness, or offensiveness 混亂
4. folklore ['foʊklɔːr] (n.) customs, beliefs, stories, and sayings of a culture handed down from generation to generation 風俗；民間故事
5. quackery ['kwækəri] (n.) the conduct of a charlatan, dishonesty 騙人的行為；騙術

9 Art

🎧 9   A current opinion, far too common, holds that art is a luxury, a monopoly[1] of wealth, a matter of museums, something to be indulged in only one's leisure, and quite inessential to and divorced from one's daily activities. How far from the truth! It is true that to understand a great painting one must look at it long and contemplatively[2]; that to understand a sonata[3] one must hear it, undistractedly[4], many times.

   Few poems reveal all their beauty and meaning in one reading. Real understanding requires concentration of eye, or ear, feeling, and intelligence. Granted[5], however, that great art is relatively rare and required contemplation and leisure for its true appreciation. Still art and a way of art permeate[6] the world in which we live.

↗ Helen Louise Gardner (1908-1986):
Art in Everyday Life ☆

Comprehension

🍁 *What does Helen Louise Gardner think about art?*

1. monopoly [mə'nɑːpəli] (n.) exclusive possession or control 獨占
2. contemplatively ['kɑːntempleɪtɪvli] (adv.) thoughtfully, meditatively 沉思地
3. sonata [sə'nɑːtə] (n.) an instrumental musical composition usually for one instrument and typically with three or four movements 奏鳴曲
4. undistractedly [ˌʌndɪ'stræktɪdli] (adv.) without distraction, without drawing attention away 專注地
5. granted ['græntɪd] (conj.) acknowledged as a supposition 就算；即使
6. permeate ['pɜːrmieɪt] (v.) to pass through, spread through 擴散；散布

10 Music

Sure there is music even in the beauty, and the silent note which Cupid strikes[1], far sweeter than the sound of an instrument. For there is music wherever there is a harmony, order or proportion; and thus far we may maintain the music of the spheres[2]; for those whose well ordered motions[3], and regular paces[4], though they give no sound unto the ear, yet to the understanding they strike a note most full of harmony.

↗ Sir Thomas Browne (1605-1682) ☆

Comprehension

🍂 *What is "music" according to Sir Thomas Browne?*
🍁 *What would be some examples of "music" based on this passage?*

1. strike [straɪk] (v.) to play an instrument by pulling on the strings or hitting the keys, such as playing the harp 演奏；敲打
2. sphere [sfɪr] (n.) the apparent surface of the heavens of which half forms the dome of the visible sky, heavens, sky, a celestial body 天空；天體
3. motion ['moʊʃən] (n.) the act of changing places or positions 運動
4. pace [peɪs] (n.) the rate of speed at which an activity or movement proceeds 速度

It is cruel, you know, that music should be so beautiful. It has the beauty of loneliness & of pain: of strength & freedom. The beauty of disappointment & never-satisfied love. The cruel beauty of nature, & everlasting[5] beauty of monotony[6].

↗ Benjamin Britten (1913-1976) ✶

The Night (Arnold Bocklin, 1827-1901)

Comprehension

🍁 *According to Britten, what are some emotions and feelings that can be expressed by music?*

🍂 *Why is music beautiful and cruel at the same time?*

5. everlasting [ˌevərˈlæstɪŋ] (a.) lasting forever, enduring through all time 永恆的
6. monotony [məˈnɑːtəni] (n.) sameness of tone or sound, lack of variation in pitch, intonation, or inflection 單音；無變化

A Sculpture Gallery (Sir Lawrence Alma-Tadema, 1836-1912)

11 | Taste and Judgment

11
How shall a man go through college without having been marked[1] for taste and judgment? What will become of him? What will his end be? They are having night schools now, you know, for college graduates. Why? Because they have not been educated enough to find their way around in contemporary[2] literature. They don't know what they may safely like in the libraries and galleries. They don't know how to judge an editorial[3] when they see one. They don't know how to judge a political campaign. They don't know when they are being fooled by a metaphor[4], an analogy[5], a parable[6]. And metaphor is, of course, what we are talking about. Education by poetry is education by metaphor.

1. mark [mɑːrk] (v.) to make a visible trace or impression on; to distinguish or characterize 留下痕跡；表示……特徵
2. contemporary [kən'tempəreri] (a.) of or in the style of the present or recent times 當代的
3. editorial [ˌedɪ'tɔːriəl] (n.) an article in a newspaper which expresses the editor's opinion on a subject of particular interest at the present time 社論；重要評論
4. metaphor ['metəfɔːr] (n.) a way of describing something by referring to it as something different and suggesting that it has similar qualities to that thing 隱喻
5. analogy [ə'nælədʒi] (n.) a comparison between things which have similar features, often used to help explain a principle or idea 類推；類比
6. parable ['pærəbəl] (n.) a simple, imagined story that teaches us a moral or spiritual lesson 寓言

The Snake Charmer (Henri Rousseau, 1844-1910)

Suppose we stop short of imagination, initiative[7], enthusiasm, inspiration and originality[8]—dread words. Suppose we don't mark in such things at all. There are still two minimal things that we have got to take care of, taste and judgment. Americans are supposed to have more judgment than taste, but taste is there to be dealt with. That is what poetry, the only art in colleges of arts, is there for.

I for my part would not be afraid to go in for enthusiasm. There is the enthusiasm like a blinding light, or the enthusiasm of the deafening[9] shout, the crude enthusiasm that you get uneducated by poetry, outside of poetry. It is exemplified[10] in what I might call "sunset raving[11]." You look westward toward the sunset, or if you get up early enough, eastward toward the sunrise, and you rave. It is oh's and ah's with you and no more.

↗ Robert Frost (1874-1963):
Education by Poetry ☀

Comprehension
_____

🍁 *According to Robert Frost, what was the purpose of studying in a college?*

🍁 *Who was Frost referring to in the passage as "they" in the first paragraph?*

🍁 *Why did Robert Frost think that Americans should have more judgment than taste?*

🍁 *What did Robert Frost think people could do to improve their taste?*

7. initiative [ɪˈnɪʃətɪv] (n.) the first of a series of actions 首創精神
8. originality [ə,rɪdʒɪˈnæləti] (n.) the state of being original, the ability to think or do something in a brand new way 原創性
9. deafening [ˈdefənɪŋ] (a.) loud enough to cause (temporary) hearing loss 震耳欲聾的
10. exemplify [ɪɡˈzemplɪfaɪ] (v.) to be a typical example of something, to show or illustrate by giving an example 舉例證明
11. rave [ˈreɪv] (v.) to talk wildly or with great enthusiasm 熱切地談論

The Poem of the Soul: The Wrong Path
(Anne-Francois-Louis Janmot, 1814-1892)

12 Time

🎧 12 The hours of a wise man are lengthened by his ideas as those of a fool are by his passions. The time of the one is long, because he does not know what to do with it; as is that of the other, because he distinguishes every moment of it with useful or amusing thoughts, or in other words, because the one is always wishing it away, and the other always enjoying it.

How different is the view of past life, in the man who is grown old in knowledge and wisdom, from that of him who is grown in ignorance and folly? The latter is like the owner of a barren country, that fills his eye with the prospect of naked hills and plains, which produce nothing either profitable or ornamental; the other beholds[1] a beautiful and spacious landscape, divided into delightful gardens, green meadows, fruitful fields, and can scarcely cast his eye upon[2] a single spot of his possessions, that is not covered with some beautiful plant or flower.

↗ Joseph Addison (1672-1719):
On the Idea of Time ✱

Comprehension

🍁 *Who was "the one?" Was it the wise man or the fool?*
🍁 *What did Addison analogize a person's past life to?*

1. behold [bɪˈhoʊld] (v.) to perceive through sight 注視
2. cast one's eye upon: to direct attention to something or someone
   視線落在⋯⋯

Wanderer Above the Sea of Fog (Caspar David Friedrich, 1774-1840)

13 Direction

🎧 13 🎧 I find the great thing in this world is not so much where we stand, as in what direction we are moving: To reach the port of heaven, we must sail sometimes with the wind[1] and sometimes against it—but we must sail, and not drift[2], nor lie at anchor[3].

↗ Oliver Wendell Holmes (1809-1894)

14 Courage

🎧14 Courage takes many forms. There is physical courage; there is moral[4] courage. Then there is a still higher type of courage—the courage to brave pain, to live with[5] it, to never let others know of it and to still find joy in life; to wake up in the morning with an enthusiasm[6] for the day ahead.

↗ Howard Cosell (1918-1995) ✦

Comprehension

🍁 *What did Oliver Holmes think would be the most important thing in this world?*

🍁 *What does the word "sail" imply?*

🍁 *What is an example of physical and moral courage?*

1. with the wind: in the direction of the wind 順風
2. drift [drɪft] (v.) (for an object) to go along with water or air; (for a person) to have no special intentions or directions 漂流
3. anchor [ˈæŋkər] (n.) a piece of heavy metal that is lowered to the bottom of the sea, lake etc. to prevent a ship or boat moving 錨
4. moral [ˈmɔːrəl] (a.) relating to the social standards of right and wrong 道德的
5. to live with: to put up with a difficult situation, accept or come to terms with, tolerate or accommodate oneself to 接受；忍受
6. enthusiasm [ɪnˈθuːziæzəm] (n.) strong excitement of feeling 熱衷；熱忱

15 The Englishman

Let me come to the point boldly: what governs the Englishman is his inner atmosphere, the weather in his soul. It is nothing particularly spiritual or mysterious. When he has taken his exercise and is drinking his tea or his beer and lighting his pipe; when, in his garden or by his fire, he sprawls[1] in an aggressively[2] comfortable chair; when, well-washed and well-brushed, he resolutely[3] turned in church to the east and recites the Creed[4] (with genuflexions[5], if he likes genuflexions) without in the least implying that he believes one word of it; when he hears or sings the

The Suitor (Walter-Dendy Sadler, 1854-1923)

most crudely sentimental and thinnest of popular songs, unmoved but not disgusted; when he makes up his mind who is his best friend or his favorite poet; when he adopts a party or a sweetheart; when he is hunting or shooting or boating, or striding[6] through the fields; when he is choosing his clothes or his profession—never is it a precise reason, or purpose, or outer fact that determines him; it is always the atmosphere of his inner man.

↗ George Santayana (1863-1952):
Soliloquies[7] in England ＊

Comprehension

🍁 *What do you think creates a person's "inner atmosphere?"*

1. sprawl [sprɔːl] (v.) to sit or lie with one's arms and legs spread out 四肢攤開
2. aggressively [əˈgresɪvli] (adv.) extremely 極度地
3. resolutely [ˈrezəluːtli] (adv.) marked by determination 堅決地
4. Creed [kriːd] (n.) the Apostles' Creed; a statement of the essential beliefs of a religious faith 使徒信條
5. genuflexion [ˌdʒenjʊˈflekʃən] (n.) the act of bending one's knees, especially in worship or reverence 屈膝膜拜
6. stride [straɪd] (v.) to walk with big, long steps 跨大步走
7. soliloquy [səˈlɪləkwi] (n.) the act of talking to one's self, especially in a play 獨白

American Gothic (Grant Wood, 1892-1942)

16 A Picture of Americans

🎧 16 It is a strange and curious picture of Americans. If ever a people had behind them a tradition of great purposes, tremendous[1] dreams, the people of America have that tradition. There is not one of us, there is not a child in this Republic, who does not know the story. The whole history of our continent[2] is a history of the imagination.

Men imagined the forests, the great plains, the rivers, the mountains—and found these plains, these mountains. No force of terror, no pressure of population, drove our ancestors[3] across this continent. They came as the great explorers crossed the Atlantic, because of the imagination of their minds—because they imagined a better, a more beautiful, a freer, happier world; because they were men not only of courage, not only of strength and hardiness, but of warm and vivid desire; because they desired; because they had the power to desire.

↗ Archibald MacLeish (1892-1982):
A Continuing Journey

Comprehension

🍁 *According to the writer, what is the most important tradition of the Americans?*

🍁 *What are some of the characteristics of the Americans?*

1. tremendous [trɪˈmendəs] (a.) considerable, remarkable; extremely large, powerful or strong 驚人的；巨大的
2. continent [ˈkɑːntɪnənt] (n.) one of the large landmasses of the earth 洲；大陸
3. ancestor [ˈænsestər] (n.) someone from whom you are descended 祖先

17 The Native Americans

🎧 17 The ancestors of Native Americans, traveling across the Bering Strait[1] from Asia, began arriving on our continent about thirty thousand years ago. By the time of Columbus[2], more than seven hundred tribes[3] lived in North America. These tribes were highly diverse[4], having different languages, shelters, religious customs, and governments.

The Native Americans were primarily hunters and gatherers. They later developed agriculture, and by 1500, corn was an important crop to many tribes. Most Native Americans were peaceful people, settling their differences through negotiation, not war.

↗ Barry Bernstein:
Literature and Language ✴

Comprehension

🍁 *Who were the first dwellers in North America?*
🍁 *Why do you think the Native Americans traveled from Asia to North America?*

1. Bering Strait: the narrowest part of the Bering Sea, which is located in the northern part of the Pacific Ocean that separates Siberia in Asia and Alaska in North America 白令海峽
2. Columbus (1451-1506): an Italian explorer and navigator working for Spain, who determined that Earth was round and discovered America in 1492 哥倫布
3. tribe [traɪb] (n.) a group of people including many families or generations with the same ethnicity 部落；種族
4. diverse [dɪˈvɜːrs] (a.) different from one another 不同的

Winold Reiss (1886-1953)

Shadows in Bedroom Corner
(Stefan Johansson, 1876-1955)

|8 Home

18   Home is where the heart is. There's no place like it. I love my home with a ferocity[1] totally out of proportion[2] to its appearance or location. I love dumb things about it: hot-water heater, the plastic rack[3] you drain[4] dishes in, the roof over my head, which occasionally leaks[5]. And yet it is precisely those dumb things that make it what it is—a place of certainty, stability[6], predictability[7], privacy[8], for me and for my family. It is where I live. What more can you say about a place than that? That is everything.

↗ Anna Quindlen (1952-):
Living Out Loud ⁕

Comprehension

🍂 *What do you think Anna Quidlen's house might have looked like? Was it a luxurious new house?*

🍁 *Why did Quindlen say the hot-water heater, the plastic racks, and the roof were dumb things?*

Sunlight
(Vilhelm Hammershoi, 1864-1916)

1. ferocity [fə'rɑːsɪti] (n.) the state of being extremely wild and turbulent 凶猛；狂暴
2. out of proportion: not in proper relation to other things, especially by being the wrong size or amount 不相稱
3. rack [ræk] (n.) a frame, stand, or structure used to hang or hold things 架子
4. drain [dreɪn] (v.) to draw off liquid completely 瀝乾；排乾（水分）
5. leak [liːk] (v.) to permit something, especially liquid, from escaping or entering through an opening 漏水
6. stability [stə'bɪləti] (n.) the state of being stable or unchanging 穩定
7. predictability [prɪˌdɪktə'bɪlɪti] (n.) the quality of being predictable or having ability to foretell on the basis of observation, experience, or scientific reason 可預測性
8. privacy ['praɪvəsi] (n.) the state or quality of being private, withdrawal from company or public view 隱私

Townsfolk Shopping Along the Oude Gracht, Utrecht (Willem Johannes Oppenoorth, 1847-1905)

19 Supermarket

I often go to the supermarket for the pure fun of it, and I suspect a lot of other people do too. The supermarket fills some of the same needs that neighborhood saloon[1] used to satisfy. There you can mix with neighbors when you are lonely, or feeling claustrophobic[2] with family, or when you simply feel the urge to get out and be part of the busy, interesting world.

Urban people, of course, are terribly scared nowadays. They may yearn[3] for society, but it is risky to go around talking to strangers, for a lot of reasons, one being that people are so accustomed[4] not to have many human contacts that they are afraid they may find out they really prefer life that way.

Whatever the reason, they go to the supermarket to be with people, but not to talk with people. The rule seems to be, you can look but you can't speak. Ah, well, most days there is a good bit to see.

↗ Russell Baker (1925-):
Small Kicks in Superland ✱

Comprehension

🍁 *According to Russell Baker, what were the similarities between a supermarket and the neighborhood saloon?*

🍁 *Is there a place where you like to go just for the pure fun of it?*

1. saloon [səˈluːn] (n.) old fashioned term for a place where liquor is sold; a drinking bar 酒館
2. claustrophobic [ˌklɔːstrəˈfoubɪk] (a.) abnormal dread of being in closed or narrow spaces 幽閉恐懼症的
3. yearn [jɜːrn] (v.) to long for something persistently 渴望
4. accustomed [əˈkʌstəmd] (a.) in the habit of or adapted to 習慣的

2 Speeches & Sayings

20 People and Liberty

[20]—You can fool all the people some of the time, and some of the people all the time, but you cannot fool all the people all of the time.

—I fear you do not fully comprehend the danger of abridging the liberties of the people. Nothing but the sternest necessity can ever justify it. A government had better go to the extreme of toleration, than to do aught[1] that could be construed into an interference[2] with, or to jeopardize[3] in any degree, the common rights of its citizens.

—Government of the people, by the people, for the people, shall not perish[4] from the Earth.

↗Abraham Lincoln (1809-1865) ✶

Comprehension

🍂 *In your own words, explain how would Lincoln like us to behave?*
🍁 *What rights do the citizens have in common? What do you think?*

1. aught [ɑːt] (n.) anything whatever 任何事物
2. interference [ˌɪntərˈfɪrəns] (n.) the act of hindering or obstructing or impeding 阻礙；干涉
3. jeopardize [ˈdʒepərdaɪz] (v.) present a danger to 冒危險
4. perish [ˈperɪʃ] (v.) to die, especially in an accident or by being killed, or to be destroyed 毀滅；死去

Martin Luther King (1929-1968)

21 | Hate and Nonviolence

21 —Like an unchecked cancer, hate corrodes[1] the personality and eats away[2] its vital[3] unity. Hate destroys a man's sense of values and his objectivity[4]. It causes him to describe the beautiful as ugly and the ugly as beautiful, and to confuse the true with the false and the false with the true.

—Nonviolence is the answer to the crucial political and moral questions of our time; the need for mankind to overcome oppression[5] and violence without resorting to[6] oppression and violence. Mankind must evolve for all human conflict a method which rejects revenge, aggression, and retaliation[7]. The foundation of such a method is love.

I have a dream
that my four little children will one day
live in a nation where
they will not be judged by the color of their skin
but by the content of their character.

—I believe that unarmed truth and unconditional love
will have the final word[8] in reality. That is why right,
temporarily defeated, is stronger than evil triumphant.

↗ Martin Luther King (1929-1968):
Strength to Love

Comprehension

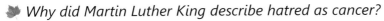

🍃 *Why did Martin Luther King describe hatred as cancer?*
🍁 *What is Nonviolence?*

---

1. corrode [kə'roʊd] (v.) to weaken or destroy gradually 侵蝕；損害
2. eat away: to wear away or destroy slowly 損壞
3. vital ['vaɪtl] (a.) characteristic of life or living beings, of crucial importance 極重要的
4. objectivity [,ɔːbdʒek'tɪvɪti] (n.) based on real facts and not influenced by personal beliefs or feelings 客觀
5. oppression [ə'prɛʃən] (n.) arbitrary and cruel exercise of power 壓迫
6. resort to: to turn to something, sometimes something extreme, for help in dealing with a problem 訴諸於
7. retaliation [rɪ,tæli'eɪʃən] (n.) to hurt someone or do something harmful to them because they have done or said something harmful to you 報復
8. have the final word: to say the last statement in a discussion or argument 最後的發言

Interior With Young Man Reading (Vilhelm Hammershoi, 1864-1916)

22 Youth

O Youth: Do you know that yours is not the first generation to yearn for a life full of beauty and freedom? Do you know that all your ancestors felt as you do—and fell victim[1] to trouble and hatred?

Do you know, also, that your fervent[2] wishes can only find fulfillment if you succeed in attaining love and understanding of men, and animals, and plants, and stars, so that every joy becomes your joy and every pain your pain?

Open your eyes, your hearts, your hands, and avoid the poison your forebears[3] so greedily sucked in[4] from history. Then will all the earth be your fatherland[5], and all your work and effort spread forth blessings.

↗ Albert Einstein (1879-1955):
Entry written in an album, 1932 ✻

Comprehension

🍁 *What does "poison" refer to in this passage?*
🍁 *What did Einstein suggest we do in order to attain happiness?*

1. fall victim: to become the victim 成為犧牲者
2. fervent ['fɜːrvənt] (a.) exhibiting a very warm or intensified feeling 熱烈的
3. forebear ['fɔːrber] (n.) ancestor, forefather 祖先
4. suck (in) to draw something, especially liquid, into the mouth 吸取
5. fatherland ['fɑːðərlænd] (n.) a person's native land or country 祖國

23 Rules of Civility[1]

1. Every action in company ought to be with some sign of respect to those present.
2. In the presence of others sing not to yourself with a humming[2] voice, nor drum with your fingers or feet.
3. Speak not when others speak; sit not when others stand, and walk not when others stop.
4. Turn not your back to others, especially in speaking; jog[3] not the table or desk on which another reads or writes; lean not on anyone.
5. Be no flatterer[4], neither play with anyone that delights not to be played with.
6. Read no letters, books, or papers in company; but when there is a necessity for doing it, you must ask leave. Come not near the books or writings of anyone so as to read them unasked; also look not nigh[5] when another is writing a letter.
7. Let your countenance[6] be pleasant, but in serious matters somewhat grave.
8. Show not yourself glad at the misfortune of another, though he were your enemy.

1. civility [sɪˈvɪlɪti] (n.) civil behavior, politeness, courtesy 禮貌；謙恭
2. hum [hʌm] (v.) to make a sound with muffled voice, to sing with closed lips 哼歌
3. jog [dʒɑːɡ] (v.) to shake or push at something slightly 輕推
4. flatterer [ˈflætərə] (n.) a person who says praises to another person without sincerity or with motives of self-interest 阿諛奉承的人
5. nigh [naɪ] (adv.) an old word for "near" 接近
6. countenance [ˈkaʊntɪnəns] (n.) facial expression 面容；臉色

9. Gaze not on the marks or blemishes[7] of others, and ask not how they came. What you may speak in secret to your friend deliver not before others.
10. Speak not in an unknown tongue in company, but in your own language; and that as those of quality do, and not as the vulgar[8]. Sublime[9] matters treat seriously.
11. Think before you speak; pronounce not imperfectly, nor bring out your words too hastily, but orderly and distinctly.
12. When another speaks, be attentive[10] yourself, and disturb not the audience. If any hesitate in his words, help him not, nor prompt[11] him without being desired; interrupt him not, nor answer him till his speech be ended.
13. Be not curious to know the affairs of others, neither approach to those that speak in private.
14. Undertake not what you cannot perform; but be careful to keep your promise.

↗ George Washington (1732-1799) ✳

---

7. blemish ['blemɪʃ] (n.) a mark of imperfection, flaws or defects that seriously impairs appearance 斑點；疤痕
8. vulgar ['vʌlgər] (a.) relating to a form of a language spoken by people generally 通俗語的
9. sublime [sə'blaɪm] (a.) grand or noble in thinking, being impressive which arouses admiration and wonder 超凡的
10. attentive [ə'tentɪv] (a.) paying close attention 專注的
11. prompt [prɑːmpt] (v.) to cause or incite someone to do something 促使；慫恿

Comprehension

🍂 *Which of the above rules of civility teaches us to respect other people's privacy?*

🍁 *Which of the above rules of civility is most important to you?*

🍂 *What are some examples of sublime matters?*

🍁 *Which of the above rules of civility teaches us to discipline ourselves?*

The Resurrection
(Jacek Malczewski, 1829-1854)

24 Sayings of Benjamin Franklin

24 1. Well done is better than well said.
2. Be civil to all; sociable to many; familiar with few; friend to one; enemy to none.
3. Be studious[1] in your profession, and you will be learned. Be industrious[2] and frugal[3], and you will be rich. Be sober[4] and temperate, and you will be healthy. Be in general virtuous[5], and you will be happy. At least, you will, by such conduct, stand the best chance for such consequences.
4. The end of Passion is the beginning of Repentance[6].
5. Dost[7] thou[8] love life? Then do not squander[9] time, for that's the stuff life is made of.
6. Remember, that time is money.
7. I have always thought that one man of tolerable[10] abilities may work great changes, and accomplish great

affairs among mankind, if he first forms a good plan, and, cutting off all amusements or other employments that would divert[11] his attention, make the execution[12] of that same plan his sole study and business.

8. At twenty years of age, the will reigns[13]; at thirty, the wit; and at forty, the judgment.

9. Admiration is the daughter of ignorance.

10. Lost time is never found again.

↗ Benjamin Franklin (1706-1790) ＊

Comprehension

🍁 *Which of the above sayings teaches us about how we should spend our time?*

🍁 *According to Franklin, do you have to be a genius in order to succeed in life? Please quote the relevant sayings.*

1. studious ['stuːdiəs] (a.) devoted to learning 勤學的
2. industrious [ɪn'dʌstriəs] (a.) assiduous in work 勤奮的
3. frugal ['fruːgəl] (a.) being economical in spending money or using material resources 節約的
4. sober ['soʊbər] (a.) not addicted to intoxicating drink, not drunk （飲酒、用藥等）有節制的
5. virtuous ['vɜːrtʃuəs] (a.) having or showing virtue, possessing good moral values 有品德的
6. repentance [rɪ'pentəns] (n.) feeling of sorrow for wrongdoing 悔恨
7. dost [dʌst] (aux.) old English for "do" 古英文的「do」
8. thou [θaʊ] (n.) old English for "you" 古英文的「you」
9. squander ['skwɑːndər] (v.) to spend money, time or use resources foolishly 浪費
10. tolerable ['tɑːlərəbəl] (a.) fairly good 還可以的；尚好的
11. divert [daɪ'vɜːrt] (v.) to take somebody's mind off something and draw attention to something else 轉移；使分心
12. execution [ˌeksɪ'kjuːʃən] (n.) the act or the process of carrying out something to its finish 執行
13. reign [reɪn] (v.) to be predominant or prevalent 支配

Spring (Ferdinand Hodler, 1853-1918)

25 Sayings of Chesterfield

25 1. Young men are apt[1] to think themselves wise enough, as drunken men are apt to think themselves sober enough.
2. Speak of the moderns without contempt[2], and of the ancients without idolatry[3].
3. Never seem wiser, nor more learned, than the people you are with. Wear your learning, like your watch, in a private pocket, and do not merely pull it out and strike it merely to show that you have one.
4. Whoever is in a hurry shows that the thing he is about is too big for him.
5. Any affectation[4] whatsoever in dress implies, in my mind, a flaw in the understanding.
6. The knowledge of the world is only to be acquired in the world, and not in a closet.

7. The aim of life is appreciation[5]; there is no sense in not appreciating things; and there is no sense in having more of them if you have less appreciation of them.
8. The vulgar man is always the most distinguished, for the very desire to be distinguished is vulgar.
9. One may understand the cosmos[6], but never the ego[7]; the self is more distant than any star.
10. There is no such thing on earth as an uninteresting subject; the only thing that can exist is an uninterested person.

↗ Philip Dormer Stanhope,
4th Earl of Chesterfield (1694-1773)

Comprehension

🍂 *Which of the above sayings teaches us to be humble?*
🍁 *According to Chesterfield, what may be some of the best ways to learn about the world?*
🍃 *Why do you think a vulgar man is always more distinguished? How do you think Chesterfield get this idea?*

1. apt [æpt] (a.) having a tendency to do something 傾向於
2. contempt [kən'tempt] (n.) the attitude of one who despises somebody or something as being low, mean, or unworthy 輕蔑；鄙視
3. idolatry [aɪ'dɑːlətri] (n.) blind or excessive devotion, worship of idols 盲目崇拜
4. affectation [ˌæfek'teɪʃən] (n.) artificial manner, pretense or behavior that is unnatural or adopted to give others a false impression 虛假的行為
5. appreciation [əˌpriːʃi'eɪʃən] (n.) grateful recognition, proper estimation or enjoyment 賞識；鑑賞
6. cosmos ['kɔːzməs] (n.) an orderly, harmonious universe（和諧的）宇宙
7. ego ['iːgoʊ] (n.) the self as distinct from others 自我

(Aubrey Beardsley, 1872-1898)

26 Sayings of Dr. Johnson

 26
1. Integrity[1] without knowledge is weak and useless, and knowledge without integrity is dangerous and dreadful[2].
2. A man ought to read just as inclination[3] leads him; for what he reads as a task[4] will do him little good.
3. Knowledge is of two kinds. We know a subject ourselves, or we know where we can find information upon it.
4. Human life is everywhere a state in which much is to be endured, and little to be enjoyed.

5. Example is always more efficacious[5] than precept[6].
6. Language is the dress of thought.
7. He is no wise man who will quit a certainty for an uncertainty.
8. Love is the wisdom of the fool and the folly[7] of the wise.

↗ Dr. Samuel Johnson (1709-1784) ✳

Comprehension

🍁 *Why is language the "dress" of thought?*
🍁 *Which of Dr. Johnson's sayings do you agree with the most? Why?*

1. integrity [ɪn'tegrəti] (n.) strict adherence to a code of moral or ethical value 正直
2. dreadful ['dredfəl] (a.) extremely unpleasant, harmful, or serious in its effects 可怕的
3. inclination [ˌɪŋklɪ'neɪʃən] (n.) a tendency toward a particular state, character, or action 傾向
4. task [tæsk] (n.) work imposed either by a person in authority or by an employer 任務；工作
5. efficacious [ˌefɪ'keɪʃəs] (a.) able to produce a desired effect 有效的
6. precept ['priːsept] (n.) a command or principle intended as a general rule of action or conduct 訓誡
7. folly ['fɑːli] (n.) foolish act or idea 愚蠢的行為

67

Francis Bacon (1561-1626)

27 Sayings of Francis Bacon

27 1. If a man will begin with certainties, he shall end in doubts; but if he will content to begin with doubts, he shall end in certainties.
2. Hope is a good breakfast, but it is a bad supper.
3. The worst solitude[1] is to be destitute[2] of sincere friendship.
4. Prosperity is not without many fears and distastes[3]; and adversity is not without comforts and hopes. Prosperity doth best discover vice[4], but adversity doth best discover virtue.
5. If a man be gracious and courteous to strangers, it shows he is a citizen of the world.
6. The inquiry[5] of truth, which is the love-making, or wooing[6] of it, the knowledge of truth, which is the presence of it, and the belief of truth, which is the enjoying of it, is the sovereign[7] good of human nature.

1. solitude ['sɑːlɪtuːd] (n.) the state of being alone without companions 孤獨；隔絕
2. destitute ['destɪtuːt] (a.) lacking something needed or desirable 缺乏的
3. distaste [dɪs'teɪst] (n.) dislike, aversion 不喜歡；憎厭
4. vice [vaɪs] (n.) a moral fault or weakness in someone's character 邪惡；不道德
5. inquiry [ɪn'kwaɪri] (n.) investigation, search for information, examination of the facts 探索；探究
6. woo [wuː] (v.) to seek, pursue, or gain; try to get the love of 追求
7. sovereign ['sɑːvrɪn] (a.) of the highest good 最高的；崇高的

Der Studierenden Selbstbildnis (Ferdinand Hodler, 1853-1918)

7. Young men are fitter to invent than to judge, fitter for execution than for counsel[8], and fitter for new projects than for settled business.
8. There is in human nature generally more of the fool than of the wise.
9. Chiefly the mould[9] of a man's fortune is in his own hands.
10. Reading maketh[10] a full man; conference a ready man and writing an exact man.

↗ Francis Bacon (1561-1626) ✴

Comprehension

🍂 *Do you agree with Sir Francis Bacon that hope is a good breakfast but a bad supper? Why or why not?*

🍁 *How can prosperity discover vice and adversity discover virtue?*

🍃 *In summary, what is the sovereign good of human nature?*
   □ *inquiry* □ *knowledge* □ *belief* □ *truth*

🍁 *What does No. 9 from the above list mean?*
   □ *A man has the equipment to print his own money.*
   □ *A man has the power to create his own wealth.*
   □ *A man already has all the money he can make.*

---

8. counsel ['kaʊnsəl] (n.) the giving of advice, the exchange of opinions and ideas 諮詢；建議
9. mould [moʊld] (n.) a form or a frame used to shape an object (British: mould; American: mold) 塑造；形成
10. maketh [mækθ] (v.) old English for "make" 「make」的古英文

Thomas Jefferson (1743-1826)

28 Sayings of Thomas Jefferson

 1. Never put off[1] till tomorrow what you can do today.
2. Never trouble another for what you can do yourself.
3. Never spend your money before you have it.
4. Never buy what you do not want, because it is cheap; it will be dear to you.
5. Pride costs us more than hunger, thirst, and cold.
6. We never repent of having eaten too little.
7. Nothing is troublesome that we do willingly.
8. How much pain have cost us the evils which have never happened.
9. Take things always by their smooth handle.
10. When angry, count ten, before you speak; if very angry, a hundred.

↗ Thomas Jefferson (1743-1826) ☆

Comprehension

🍁 *Which of Jefferson's sayings is applicable to your life?*
🍁 *What does the word "evils" mean in No. 8 on the above list?*
   □ *something that causes suffering, sorrow, and trouble*
   □ *of the ghosts and monsters*
   □ *bad and ugly things*

1. put off: to postpone, delay 延期

All Saints' Day (Emile Friant, 1863-1932)

29 Thoughts About Life

🎧 **29** A good reputation is better than expensive perfume; and the day you die is better than the day you are born.

It is better to go to a home where there is mourning than to one where there is a party, because the living should always remind themselves that death is waiting for us all.

Sorrow is better than laughter; it may sadden[1] your face, but it sharpens[2] your understanding.

Someone who is always thinking about happiness is a fool. A wise person thinks about death.

It is better to have wise people reprimand[3] you than to have stupid people sing your praises.

↗ Good News Bible: *Ecclesiastes: 7: 1-5* ✶

Comprehension

🍁 *Do you agree with the messages in this passage? Why?*

🍁 *What does the word "evils" mean in No. 8 on the above list?*
a. something that causes suffering, sorrow, and trouble
b. of the ghosts and monsters
c. bad and ugly things

1. sadden ['sædn] (v.) to make one sad 使悲傷
2. sharpen ['ʃɑːrpən] (v.) to improve something so that it is more efficient or stylish than before 使敏銳
3. reprimand ['reprɪmænd] (v.) to criticize a person severely for something he or she has done, usually by a person of authority 訓斥；斥責

The Land of Cockayne (Pieter the Elder Bruegel, 1525-1569)

30 Warning

🎧 30 Lazy people should learn a lesson from the way ants live. They have no leader, chief, or ruler, but they store up[1] their food during the summer, getting ready for winter. How long is the lazy man going to lie around[2]? When is he ever going to get up?

"I'll just take a short nap[3]," he says; "I'll fold my hands and rest a while."

But while he sleeps, poverty will attack him like an armed robber[4].

↗ Good News Bible: *Proverbs: 6: 6-15* ✲

Comprehension

🍁 *According to the passage, what are the differences between lazy people and ants?*

🍁 *Why did the writer analogize poverty to an armed robber?*

1. store up: to accumulate something for future use 貯存
2. lie around: not to do anything productive, hang around idly 無所事事地閒晃
3. nap [næp] (n.) a short period of light sleep during the day 午睡；小睡
4. robber ['rɑːbər] (n.) a thief who steals from someone by threatening violence 強盜；搶犯

The Money Lender And His Wife
(Quentin Massys, ca.1465-1530)

3 | Money

If you love money, you will never be satisfied; if you long[1] to be rich, you will never get all you want. It is useless. The richer you are, the more mouths you have to feed[2]. All you gain is the knowledge that you are rich. A working man may or may not have enough to eat, but at least he can get a good night's sleep. A rich man, however, has so much that he stays awake worrying.

↗ Good News Bible:
Ecclesiastes: 5: 10-12 *

Death and the Miser (Hieronymus Bosch, ca.1453-1516)

Comprehension

🍁 *What kind of lifestyle is this passage promoting?*

🍂 *If you could choose, would you rather be rich or poor?*

---

1. long [lɔːŋ] (v.) to feel a strong desire or craving for something, especially for something not likely to be attained 渴望
2. feed [fiːd] (v.) to provide or supply food for another (feed → fed → fed) 餵食；供給食物

3 Biographies & Diaries

Mahatma Gandhi (1869-1948)

32 Mahatma Gandhi

32 Gandhi's great aim in life was to help to improve the conditions of poor and suffering people, and to aid his people in any way he could, but always without using force. He was against every sort of evil, no matter of what kind. When he tried to find out about the conditions among poor farm workers, the people crowded around him by the hundreds. A friend had come among them, someone who wanted to help them, and to them this was something new. When the police ordered Gandhi to leave the place, he refused, and in court he explained why he could not obey. Then he asked the court to punish him for breaking the law.

The court did not know what to do with such a man, and so they let him go free. This was the first step in what came to be an important and common event in many parts of India—to refuse to obey a law considered to be unjust, and at the same time calmly to accept any punishment that might be given.

↗ Leslie W. Leavitt:
Great Men and Women ✳

Comprehension
_____

🍁 *What do you think Gandhi said to the court to explain why he broke the laws?*

🍁 *Why do you think Gandhi accept the punishment even though he thought the laws were unjust?*

Isaac Newton (1643-1727)

33 Scientist

🎧 33 I do not know what I may appear to the world, but to myself I seem to have been only like a boy playing on the seashore, and diverting myself in now and then finding a smoother pebble[1] or a prettier shell than ordinary, whilst[2] the great ocean of truth lay all undiscovered before me.

↗ Isaac Newton (1643-1727):
Memoirs[3] of Newton ✵

Comprehension

🍁 *What was Newton referring to in this passage?*
  a. His life as a boy.
  b. His favorite pastime.
  c. The fact that he is still ignorant of many things.
  d. He wanted to swim when he was a boy, but he didn't know how.

1. pebble ['pebəl] (n.) little round stone 小圓石
2. whilst [waɪlst] (conj.) while 當
3. memoir ['memwɑːr] (n.) (usually used in plural) a story about a person's own life or told from personal experience 自傳；回憶錄

34 Albert Einstein

As Albert grew he seemed slow to learn, and this worried his parents. He was nine years old before he could express ideas clearly. But at an early age he had a very curious mind. When he was five, his father gave him a compass. How surprised his parents were to see Albert's excitement at how the compass[1] worked. This was the beginning of his lifelong love of science.

Although Albert would someday be a famous scientist, he did not like school. In the Germany of his time, school rules were strict[2] and teachers were as stern[3] as army officers. He often did poorly, for he didn't like studying things that did not interest him. Only his history teacher understood this independent student.

Einstein was indeed a puzzle. But without this great and complex[4] man's contributions to the scientific world, we would not have gained the understanding we have today of time, space, matter[5], and energy. Still, even today, we do not truly understand what this remarkable[6] man gave to the world of science.

↗ P. Z. Bradbury:
Albert Einstein ✶

🍁 *What do you think was Einstein's best subject in school?*

🍁 *Can you give an example of another great man who did not like school?*

🍁 *Are you inspired by Einstein's story? In what way?*

1. compass ['kʌmpəs] (n.) a small hand-held device used to determine directions for north, south, east and west 指南針
2. strict [strɪkt] (a.) having high standards, requiring exact and absolute compliance 嚴格的
3. stern [stɜːrn] (a.) harsh, severe, firm, unyielding, uncompromising 嚴厲的
4. complex ['kɑːm'plɛks] (a.) having many interconnected portions which make something difficult to understand 複雜的
5. matter ['mætər] (n.) a physical thing that takes up space, a substance 物質；物體
6. remarkable [rɪ'mɑːrkəbəl] (a.) attracting notice because of something unusual 不凡的

35 Marie Curie in the Laboratory

🎧 35 At home, Marie, the wife and mother, bathed her baby daughter and did the work of the house. In the laboratory, Marie, the scientist, was making one of the most important discoveries of science. A few years before, a certain scientist had discovered that a metal called uranium gave a kind of radiation[1], which Marie Curie was later to call radioactivity[2]. But where did this radiation come from and what was it like? Here was a secret of nature which she set out[3] to discover. Only a scientist could understand all that this pursuit[4] meant.

Marie Curie (1867-1934)

The experiments were done most carefully again and again. There was failure, success, more failure, a little success, a little more success, more failure, a little success, a little more success. She repeated her experiments once, twice, ten times, twenty times. All seemed to prove[5] that in the mineral which she was examining there was something, some form of radiation which man knew nothing about.

Four years before this, Marie had expressed her thoughts in words much like these: Life is not easy for any of us. We must work, and above all we must believe in ourselves. We must believe that each one of us is able to do something well, and that, when we discover what this something is, we must work until we succeed.

↗ Leslie W. Leavitt:
Great Men and Women *

Comprehension

🍂 *How many roles did Marie Curie have both inside her family and in her professional life?*

🍁 *Why do you think Marie Curie was a successful scientist?*

1. radiation [ˌreɪdɪˈeɪʃen] (n.) the combined processes of emission, transmission, and absorption of radiant energy 放射線；輻射能
2. radioactivity [ˌreɪdioʊækˈtɪvɪti] (n.) the emission of radiation by unstable elements such as uranium, plutonium, or thorium; some elements spontaneously emit energetic particles (as electrons or alpha particles) because of the disintegration of their atomic nuclei 放射能；放射現象
3. set out: to begin an earnest attempt 開始從事；著手
4. pursuit [pərˈsuːt] (n.) the act of striving toward a goal 追求
5. prove [pruːv] (v.) to demonstrate as having a particular quality or worth 證明

Benjamin Franklin (1706-1790)

36 Benjamin Franklin

When Benjamin Franklin died, the largest crowd the country had ever seen gathered in Philadelphia for his funeral[1]. The multitalented Franklin was a world-famous publisher, inventor, statesman[2], and writer, a man whose rise from poverty[3] to riches and fame[4] represented the promise of America.

Franklin came from a large and poor Boston family and had to earn his own living at an early age. When he was twelve, he became the apprentice[5] of his older brother, a printer. When he was seventeen, he ran away to Philadelphia, where he eventually owned and operated his own printing business. At twenty-four he was publishing *Poor Richard's Almanac.*

1. funeral ['fjuːnərəl] (n.) a ceremony held for a dead person usually before burial 葬禮
2. statesman ['steɪtsmən] (n.) a person skillful in dealing with matters concerning public issues, politics, and state affairs; especially, one actively engaged in conducting the business of a government or in shaping its policies 政治家
3. poverty ['pɑːvərti] (n.) being poor, the state of lacking in the usual or socially acceptable amount of money or material possessions 貧窮;貧困
4. fame [feɪm] (n.) popular acclaim, good reputation 名望
5. apprentice [ə'prentɪs] (n.) a person who is learning a trade by working for a skilled and experienced person 學徒

Benjamin Franklin Drawing Electricity From the Sky
(Benjamin West, 1738-1820)

Franklin's success enabled him to retire early and to devote himself to public service, politics, science, and inventing. His accomplishments[6] included founding[7] the University of Pennsylvania, performing important experiments with electricity, and inventing bifocals[8], the lightning rod, and the Franklin stove. Franklin never patented or profited from any of his inventions, preferring to contribute them freely in an effort to better the human condition.

↗ Barry Bernstein:
Literature and Language ✳

Comprehension

🍁 *In what ways did Benjamin Franklin inspire the American people?*
🍁 *In your opinion, what was Benjamin Franklin's greatest contribution to the world?*

6. accomplishment [əˈkɑːmplɪʃmənt] (n.) something accomplished or done successfully; achievement 成就
7. found [faʊnd] (v.) to take the first step in building or starting something 設立
8. bifocals [ˈbaɪfoʊkəlz] (n.) a pair of eyeglasses which have two focal lengths, with the upper part for distance vision and the lower part for close vision 遠近雙焦點眼鏡

The Old Stage Coach (Eastman Johnson, 1824-1906)

37 Ambition

🎧37　When I was a boy, there was but one permanent[1] ambition among my comrades[2] in our village on the west bank of the Mississippi River: that was to be a steamboatman[3]. We had transient[4] ambitions of other sorts, but they were only transient.

1. permanent ['pɜːrmənənt] (a.) continuing or enduring without fundamental or marked change 永久的
2. comrade ['kɑːmræd] (n.) a friend or companion in an activity 同伴
3. steamboatman ['stiːmboʊtmən] (n.) a person who works on a boat driven by steam 汽船水手
4. transient ['trænʃənt] (a.) lasting only a short time, short in duration 片刻的；短暫的

When a circus came and went, it left us all burning[5] to become clowns; the first Negro[6] minstrel show[7] that ever came to our section[8] left us all suffering to try that kind of life; now and then we had a hope that if we lived and were good, God would permit us to be pirates. These ambitions faded[9] out, each in its turn; but the ambition to be a steamboatman always remained.

↗ Mark Twain (1835-1910):
Autobiography ✦

↗ Mark Twain (1835-1910):
Autobiography ✦

Comprehension

🍁 *What were some of your transient ambitions?*

🍁 *What do you think roused Mark Twain's ambition to be a steamboatman?*

5. burning [ˈbɜːrnɪŋ] (a.) strongly desiring to have or to do something 熱切的
6. Negro [ˈniːɡroʊ] (n.) a member of a race of human native to Africa and classified according to their dark skin (Note: Today this word is offensive and no longer used.) 黑人；黑鬼（註：該字帶有強烈歧視意味，今日已不再使用）
7. minstrel show: a group of entertainers who paint their faces and hands black and would sing, dance and tell jokes 白人扮演黑人的滑稽表演
8. section [ˈsekʃən] (n.) a distinct part of a territory, a political area or community 區域
9. fade [feɪd] (v.) to sink away, become weaker, disappear 逐漸消失

Mark Twain (middle), George Alfred Townsend (left), and David Gray (right)

Five Boys on a Wall (Eastman Johnson, 1824-1906)

38 My Uncle John's Home

My Uncle John was a farmer, and his farm was four miles from my home in Florida, a town in Missouri. I spent part of every year at the farm until I was twelve or thirteen years old. The life which I led there with my eight cousins was delightful[1], and so is the memory of it . . .

I can recall[2] the solemn[3] twilight[4] and mystery of the deep woods, the earthy[5] smells, the faint[6] odors[7] of wild flowers, the sheen[8] of rain-washed leaves, the clatter[9] of drops when the gusts[10] shook the trees, the far-off hammering[11] of woodpeckers[12], the snapshot[13] glimpses[14] of wild creatures scurrying[15] through the grass. I can call it all back and make it as real as it ever was.

How d'ye (John George Brown, 1831-1913)

I can see the woods in their autumn dress and hear the rustle we made as we ran through the fallen leaves. I can see the blue clusters[16] of wild grapes, and I remember the taste of them and the smell. I know how the wild blackberries tasted, and the hazel nuts; and I can feel the thumping[17] rain, upon my head, of hickory nuts and walnuts when the wind sent them down.

↗ Mark Twain (1835-1910): *Autobiography* *

Comprehension

🍁 *Where was Uncle John's farm? Was it near _____?*
   a. Miami, Florida?
   b. the state of New York?
   c. a town in Florida?
   d. a town in Missouri?
🍂 *When did Mark Twain most likely visit Uncle John's farm?*

1. delightful [dɪ'laɪtfəl] (a.) very pleasing 令人欣喜的
2. recall ['riːkɔːl] (v.) to bring back to mind 回憶
3. solemn ['sɑːləm] (a.) dark, gloomy, somber 陰暗的；莊嚴的
4. twilight ['twaɪlaɪt] (n.) the time of day just after sunset or before dawn, when the Sun is below horizon 黎明；黃昏
5. earthy ['ɜːrθi] (a.) of, relating, or resembling the earth 泥土的；土地的
6. faint [feɪnt] (a.) lacking clarity or distinctiveness 微弱的；模糊的
7. odor ['oʊdər] (n.) a sensation, stimulation, or perception of the sense of smell, a smell whether pleasant or unpleasant (British: odour; American: odor) 味道；香氣
8. sheen [ʃiːn] (n.) brightness, shininess 光輝；光澤
9. clatter ['klætər] (n.) a rattling sound of hard objects striking against each other 隆隆聲
10. gust [gʌst] (n.) a strong and sudden burst of wind 一陣狂風
11. hammering ['hæmərɪŋ] (n.) the act of pounding 捶打敲擊
12. woodpecker ['wʊd,pekər] (n.) a kind of bird that falls into the Picidae family, which has stiff spiny tail feathers used in climbing or resting on tree trunks, a usually extensile tongue, and a very hard bill used to drill the bark or wood of trees for insect food or to excavate nesting cavities 啄木鳥
13. snapshot ['snæpʃɑːt] (n.) an impression, observation or view of something brief or transitory 快照
14. glimpse [glɪmps] (n.) a quick view or look 瞥視
15. scurry ['skɜːri] (v.) to move quickly (scurry → scurried → scurried) 疾行
16. cluster ['klʌstər] (n.) a group of similar things gathered together or growing together 串
17. thumping [θʌmpɪŋ] (a.) sound that's heavy and dull 發出重擊聲的

Dit is een foto, zoals
ik me zou wensen,
altijd zo te zijn.
Dan had ik nog wel
een kans. om naar
Holywood te komen.
Annefrank.
10 Oct. 1942

(translation)
"This is a photo as I would wish
myself to look all the time. Then
I would maybe have a chance to
come to Hollywood."
Anne Frank, 10 Oct. 1942

▲This is a photo as I would wish
myself to look at the time.
Then I would maybe have a
chance to come to Hollywood.

◀ Anne Frank, 10 Oct. 1942

39 Adversity[1]

🎧 39 I have often been downcast[2], but never in despair[3]; I regard our hiding as a dangerous adventure, romantic and interesting at the same time. In my diary I treat all the privations[4] as amusing. I have made up my mind now to lead a different life from other girls and, later on, different from ordinary housewives. My start has been so very full of interest, and that is the sole[5] reason why I have to laugh at the humorous side of the most dangerous moments.

↗ Anne Frank (1929-1945):
The Diary of a Young Girl ✦

Comprehension

🍂 *What would the writer recommend to someone facing adversity?*
🍁 *How do you usually react in response to adversities?*

1. adversity [ədˈvɜːrsɪti] (n.) being in a difficult and unhappy situation
   逆境；困苦
2. downcast [ˈdaʊnkæst] (a.) to feel low, depressed, discouraged
   意志消沉的
3. despair [dɪˈsper] (n.) loss of hope 絕望
4. privation [praɪˈveɪʃən] (n.) the condition of lacking the basic necessities
   of life 窮困；匱乏
5. sole [soʊl] (a.) the only one 唯一的；僅有的

40 Growing Up

40 They mustn't know my despair. I can't let them see the wounds which they have caused. I couldn't bear their sympathy and their kind-hearted jokes. It would only make me want to scream all the more. If I talk, everyone thinks I'm showing off; when I'm silent, they think I'm ridiculous; rude if I answer, sly[1] if I get a good idea, lazy if I'm tired, selfish if I eat a mouthful more than I should, stupid, cowardly, crafty[2], etc. etc.

↗ Anne Frank (1929-1945):
The Diary of a Young Girl ✲

Comprehension

🍁 *Who or what does the word "they" refer to?*

1. sly [slaɪ] (a.) cleverly skillful and cunning 狡猾的
2. crafty ['kræfti] (a.) adept in the use of subtlety and cunning, skillful in deception 狡獪的

4 Stories & Fables

4| A Child's Dream of a Star

41   There was once a child, and he strolled[1] about a good deal, and thought of a number of things. He had a sister, who was a child too, and his constant[2] companion.

These two used to wonder all day long. They wondered at the beauty of the flowers; they wondered at the height and blueness of the sky; they wondered at the depth of the bright water; they wondered at the goodness and the power of God who made the lovely world.

They used to say to one another, sometimes, supposing all the children upon earth were to die, would the flowers, and the water, and the sky be sorry?

108

Leon Frederic (1856-1940)

They believed they would be sorry. For, they said, the buds are the children of the flowers, and the little playful streams that gambol down the hillsides are the children of the water; and the smallest bright specks[3] playing at hide-and-seek in the sky all night, must surely be the children of the stars; and they would all be grieved[4] to see their playmates, the children of men, no more.

There was one clear, shining star that used to come out in the sky before the rest, near the church spire[5], above the graves. It was larger and more beautiful, they thought, than all the others, and every night they watched for it, standing hand in hand at a window. Whoever saw it first, cried out, "I see the star!"

And often they cried out both together, knowing so well when it would rise, and where. So they grew to be such friends with it, that, before lying down in their beds, they always looked out once again, to bid it good night; and when they were turning round to sleep, they used to say, "God bless the star!"

↗ Charles Dickens (1812-1870) ⁎

Peter Pan

Comprehension

In addition to the types of children mentioned in the reading, what kinds of children are there on Earth?

In this reading, how many people does the word "they" refer to? (Look for words in the story that hint to the number of characters in the story.)

Is there someone who you must bid good night to before you go to bed every night?

1. stroll [stroʊl] (v.) to walk slowly and leisurely 漫步；遊蕩
2. constant [ˈkɑːnstənt] (a.) unchanged, faithful, dependable
   不變的；忠實的
3. speck [spek] (n.) a small spot; a small amount 微粒
4. grieve [griːv] (v.) to feel sad 憂傷；悲哀
5. spire [spaɪr] (n.) a tall, pointy structure like a tower that is usually built
   on a church 教堂的尖塔

42 Growing Up

At six she had been told she was a big girl now. She was excited about going to school. She clutched[1] hard the hand of the grownup that held hers as they went up the steps of the big building, through the door, and to the entrance[2] of the classroom; then she had to let go[3], had to face that room full of children, some few she knew but many she had never seen before.

Time went by and it was her tenth birthday that was being celebrated. Even bigger was the day when she entered the teens.

There were other great occasions. To be sixteen was one, and then to be twenty-one: a grownup who could vote, a young woman who could take her own stand. Each stage of growing had blended[4] into the next effortlessly[5], inevitably[6]. Yes, always there would be something ahead. This was the learning that was life; and the savor[7], too.

↗ Elizabeth Yates (1905-2001):
Always Ahead ⁕

Comprehension

🍂 *What was so special to the writer about her 6th, 10th, 16th and the 21st birthdays?*

🍁 *What is the age range for a teenager?*

1. clutch [klʌtʃ] (v.) to grasp and hold tightly; seize 緊抓住
2. entrance ['entrəns] (n.) a door or a place for entry 門；入口
3. let go: to release or loose hold of something or someone 放手
4. blend [blend] (v.) to combine or associate so that the separate constituents are indistinguishable from one another 混合；交融
5. effortlessly ['efərtləsli] (adv.) requiring little or no effort 不費力地
6. inevitably [ɪ'nevɪtəbli] (adv.) in such a manner that is unavoidable, bound to happen without exceptions 必然地
7. savor ['seɪvər] (n.) a distinct quality or sensation 風味；滋味

43 The Black Cat

EDGAR ALLAN POE (1809-1849)

From my infancy I was noted for the docility[1] and humanity of my disposition[2]. My tenderness of heart was even so conspicuous[3] as to make me the jest[4] of my companions. I was especially fond of animals, and was indulged[5] by my parents with a great variety of pets.

With these I spent most of my time, and never was so happy as when feeding and caressing[6] them. This peculiarity[7] of character[8] grew with my growth, and, in my manhood, I derived[9] from it one of my principal[10] sources of pleasure.

To those who have cherished an affection[11] for a faithful and sagacious[12] dog, I need hardly be at the trouble of explaining the nature of the intensity of the gratification[13] thus derivable. There is something in the unselfish and self-sacrificing love of a brute[14], which goes directly to the heart of him who has had frequent occasion to test the paltry[15] friendship and gossamer[16] fidelity[17] of mere Man.

↗ Edgar Allan Poe (1809-1849):
The Black Cat ☆

🍁 *Who does the word "brute" refer to? Is it the pet or the writer himself?*

🍁 *Does the writer prefer to spend time with his pets or with his friends?*

🍁 *What does the writer think about people in general?*

1. docility [dɑː'sɪlɪti] (n.) the quality of being agreeable and easy to manage 溫順；馴良
2. disposition [ˌdɪspə'zɪʃən] (n.) a person's usual attitude toward something during a period of time 性情
3. conspicuous [kən'spɪkjuəs] (a.) noticeable, attracting attention 出色的；引人注目的
4. jest [dʒest] (n.) someone who is made fun of or teased by other people 嘲笑的對象；笑柄
5. indulge [ɪn'dʌldʒ] (v.) to give in to one's desires for doing something excessively, which is usually bad for the person 縱容；放縱
6. caress [kə'res] (v.) to touch or stroke softly and lovingly 撫摸
7. peculiarity [pɪˌkjuːli'ærɪti] (n.) something different from the usual; odd characteristics 特殊；特質
8. character ['kærɪktər] (n.) an attribute, trait, or distinctive feature that distinguishes one person from the other 性格；特質
9. derive [dɪ'raɪv] (v.) to get, receive something from a source 得到
10. principal ['prɪnsɪpəl] (a.) the most important, first-rank 首要的；主要的
11. affection [ə'fekʃən] (n.) love, liking 感情；喜愛
12. sagacious [sə'geɪʃəs] (a.) sharp, skillful, observant 聰敏的；伶俐的
13. gratification [ˌgrætɪfɪ'keɪʃen] (n.) great satisfaction 快慰；滿足
14. brute [bruːt] (n.) an animal, a beast 野獸
15. paltry ['pɔːltri] (a.) not important 不重要的；瑣碎的
16. gossamer ['gɑːsəmər] (a.) very light, delicate and filmy 薄弱的；極薄的
17. fidelity [fɪ'deləti] (n.) truthfulness and faithfulness 忠實

44 Old Town in America

🎧44 There was once a town in the heart of America where all life seemed to live in harmony with its surroundings. The town lay in the midst of a checkerboard[1] of prosperous farms, with fields of grain and hillsides of orchards[2] where, in spring, white clouds of bloom drifted above the green fields. In autumn, oak[3] and maple[4] and birch[5] set up a blaze[6] of color that flamed and flickered[7] across a backdrop[8] of pines[9]. Then foxes barked in the hills and deer silently crossed the fields, half hidden in the mists of the fall mornings.

↗ Rachel Carson (1907-1964):
Silent Spring ✲

Comprehension

🍃 *In this town, what might have been some of the things that their people could sell for a living?*

🍁 *Can you describe the town you live in?*

1. checkerboard ['tʃekərbɔːrd] (n.) something divided in equal squares like the board used to play checkers 棋盤
2. orchard ['ɔːrtʃərd] (n.) an area of land where fruit or nut trees are grown 果園
3. oak [oʊk] (n.) any of a genus (Quercus) of large hardwood trees and bushes of the beech family, bearing acorns 橡樹
4. maple ['meɪpəl] (n.) a type of large tree which grows in northern areas of the world, or the wood of this tree 楓樹
5. birch [bɜːrtʃ] (n.) a slender hardy tree having a peeling, typically silver-grey or white, bark and yielding a hard fine-grained wood 白樺樹
6. blaze [bleɪz] (n.) great brightness 光輝；燦爛
7. flicker ['flɪkər] (v.) to shine with a fluctuating light （光的）搖曳；明滅
8. backdrop ['bækdrɑːp] (n.) setting, background 背景
9. pine [paɪn] (n.) an evergreen tree that grows in cooler areas of the world 松樹

45 The Way to Rainy Mountain

A single knoll[1] rises out of the plain in Oklahoma, north and west of the Wichita Range. For my people, the Kiowas[2], it is an old landmark, and they gave it the name Rainy Mountain.

The hardest weather in the world is there. Winter brings blizzards[3], hot tornadic[4] winds arise in the spring, and in summer the prairie is an anvil[5]'s edge. The grass turns brittle[6] and brown, and it cracks[7] beneath your feet. There are green belts along the rivers and creeks, linear[8] groves[9] of hickory and pecan[10], willow[11] and witch hazel[12]. At a distance in July or August the steaming foliage[13] seems almost writhe[14] in fire. Great green and yellow grasshoppers are everywhere in the tall grass, popping up like corn to sting the flesh, and tortoises crawl about on the red earth, going nowhere in the plenty of time.

1. knoll [noʊl] (n.) a small round hill 小圓丘
2. Kiowas: a tribe of American Indians who migrated from what now is Canada to their present location in southwest Oklahoma 來自現今位於加拿大地區的印第安種族，人口多分布於奧克拉荷馬州
3. blizzard ['blɪzərd] (n.) a long and severe snowstorm 暴風雪
4. tornadic [tɔːr'neɪdɪk] (a.) of or with the characteristics of a tornado, which is a violent and destructive whirling wind that forms a funnel shape and travels in a narrow path 似颶風的；像龍捲風的
5. anvil ['ænvɪl] (n.) an heavy iron block which is used as a platform on which pieces of metal are hammered into shape 鋼砧
6. brittle ['brɪtl] (a.) hard and dry but easily broken or snapped 脆的；易碎的

119

Loneliness is an aspect of the land. All things in the plain were isolated; there is no confusion of objects in the eye, but one hill or one tree or one man. To look upon that landscape in the early morning, with the sun at your back, is to lose the sense of proportion. Your imagination comes to life, and this, you think, is where Creation was begun.

↗ N. Scott Momaday (1934-):
The Way to Rainy Mountain

🍁 *What are the "green belts" along the rivers and creeks?*

🍁 *Why did the writer say you would "lose your sense of proportion" when you look at the landscape in the early morning?*

🍁 *What does the word "Creation" refer to?*

7. crack [kræk] (v.) to cause something to break with a sudden sharp sound 裂開；破裂

8. linear ['lɪniər] (a.) consisting of a straight line 直線的

9. grove [grouv] (n.) a group of fruit or nut trees 樹叢

10. pecan [pɪˈkɑːn] (n.) an edible nut in the hickory family (Carya illinoensis) that has an oval shape and a thin shell and is widely grown in the warmer parts of the U.S. and in Mexico 美洲薄殼胡桃

11. willow ['wɪloʊ] (n.) any of a genus of trees (Salix of the family Salicaceae) with narrow leaves and flexible twigs and grows at the waterside 柳樹

12. witch hazel (n.) any of a genus (Hamamelis) of small North American and Asiatic trees and shrubs with small yellow flowers that bloom in the late fall or very early spring 北美金縷梅

13. foliage ['foʊlɪɪdʒ] (n.) leaves of plants collectively 葉子；簇葉

14. writhe [raɪð] (v.) to twist and turn this way and that way 扭動

46 Long Journey for School

46   By walking, begging rides both in wagons and in the cars, in some way, after a number of days, I reached the city of Richmond, Virginia, about eighty-two miles from Hampton. When I reached there, tired, hungry, and dirty, it was late in the night. I had never been in a large city, and this rather added to my misery[1]. When I reached Richmond, I was completely out of money. I had not a single acquaintance[2] in the place, and, being unused to city ways, I did not know where to go. I applied at several places for lodging[3], but they all wanted money, and that was what I did not have.

Knowing nothing else better to do, I walked the streets. In doing this I passed by many food stands where fried chicken and half-moon apple pies were piled[4] high and made to present a most tempting[5] appearance.

At that time it seemed to me that I would have promised all that I expected to possess in the future to have gotten hold of one of those chicken legs or one of those pies. But I could not get either of these, nor anything else to eat.

↗ Booker T. Washington (1856-1915):
Up From Slavery[6] ★

Comprehension

🍁 *What is the important lesson from this passage?*

1. misery ['mɪzəri] (n.) a state of suffering, distress, and unhappiness 悲慘；苦難
2. acquaintance [ə'kweɪntəns] (n.) a person whom one knows, but not intimately, the state or relation of being acquainted with someone 認識的人
3. lodging ['lɑːdʒɪŋ] (n.) a temporary place to live and sleep 住宿的場所
4. pile [paɪl] (v.) to heap in abundance, place a mass of things together 堆；累積
5. tempting ['temptɪŋ] (a.) attractive and able to arouse desire, having strong appeal 誘人的
6. slavery ['sleɪvəri] (n.) the state of being bound to servitude as a chattel of another person 奴隸（身分、狀態）

47 We Travel Towards The Moon

47 We passed the time[1] sleeping, reading and playing games. I used the radio to talk to my mother and father on Earth. They were worried. They said that they had read about the accident in the newspapers. I told them that there was nothing to worry about. As we traveled nearer to the Moon, I watched it through the windows. I could see the tiny towns, the mountains and the large empty fields that stretched[2] for thousands of miles.

It was exciting to see the other side of the Moon, the side that we can't see from Earth. As we traveled round the Moon, the Earth disappeared from sight. It was the first time that I hadn't been able to see the Earth. It felt strange. I could only see the sun, the moon and the stars.

↗ Arthur C. Clarke (1917-2008):
Islands in the Sky ✴

Comprehension

🍁 *Who were "we?" What was their occupation?*
🍁 *Where were those people traveling?*

---

1. pass the time: to spend time with no intended purpose 打發時間
2. stretch [stretʃ] (v.) to extend 伸長；延伸

The Goose (Berthe Morisot, 1841-1895)

48 The Very Proper Gander

Not so very long ago there was a very fine gander[1]. He was strong and smooth and beautiful and he spent most of his time singing to his wife and children.

One day somebody who saw him strutting[2] up and down in his yard and singing remarked, "There is a very proper gander."

An old hen overheard this and told her husband about it that night in the roost[3]."They said something about propaganda[4]," she said.

"I have always suspected that," said the rooster, and he went around the barnyard[5] next day telling everybody that the very fine gander was a dangerous bird, more than likely a hawk[6] in gander's clothing.

A small brown hen remembered a time when at a great distance she had seen the gander talking with some hawks in the forest. "They were up to no good[7]," she said.

A duck remembered that the gander had once told him he did not believe anything. "He said to heck with[8] the flag, too," said the duck.

A guinea hen[9] recalled that she had once seen somebody who looked very much like the gander throw something that looked like a bomb.

Finally, everybody snatched[10] up sticks and stones and descended[11] on the gander's house. He was strutting in his front yard, singing to his children and his wife.

"There he is!" everybody cried. "Hawk-lover! Unbeliever! Flag-hater! Bomb-thrower!" So they set upon him and drove him out of the country.

↗ James Thurber (1894-1961):
Fables for Our Time ✳

Edgar Hunt

🍁 *What is the moral of this story?*

1. gander ['gændər] (n.) an adult male goose 雄鵝
2. strut [strʌt] (v.) to walk in a stiff proud way 昂首闊步
3. roost [ruːst] (n.) a place where birds sleep 棲木；窩
4. propaganda [ˌprɑːpə'gændə] (n.) an organized scheme to promote an idea or a practice in order to further one's cause or to damage an opposing cause 宣傳計畫
5. barnyard ['bɑːrnjɑːrd] (n.) a usually fenced area that is next to or adjoining a barn 穀倉邊的場地
6. hawk [hɔːk] (n.) a large bird that hunts and eats small birds and animals 鷹；隼
7. up to no good (expression): planning on or doing something bad 計畫做壞事
8. to heck with . . . (expression): not to be concerned with 不甩
9. guinea hen (n.): a female African bird with a featherless head, rounded body, and dark gray feathers that are spotted with white; guinea hens are sometimes raised for food 雌珠雞
10. snatch [snætʃ] (v.) to take, grasp, or seize something abruptly, quickly, or hastily 抓住
11. descend [dɪ'send] (v.) to make sudden attack on 突然襲擊

William Holbrook Beard (1825-1900)

49 A Fable

The sages of antiquity[1] kindly invented a way of telling people the truth without being rude to their faces: They held before them a singular mirror in which all kinds of animals and strange things came into view, and produced a spectacle[2] as entertaining as it was edifying[3]. They called it "A Fable," and whatever foolish or intelligent thing the animals performed there, the human beings had but to apply it to themselves and thereby think: the fable alludes[4] to you.

↗ Hans Christian Andersen (1805-1875):
Anderse's Fairy Tales ☆

Comprehension

🍁 *What is an example of a fable? Can you remember a good one that alludes to you?*

1. antiquity [æn'tɪkwɪti] (n.) ancient times 古代
2. spectacle ['spektəkəl] (n.) an amazing scene or view 場面；奇觀
3. edifying ['edɪfaɪɪŋ] (a.) improving your mind 有教化意味的
4. allude [ə'luːd] (v.) to hint about something without saying it directly 略為提及；暗指

5 Poems

50 A Grain of Sand

To see a World in a Grain of Sand,
And a Heaven in a Wild Flower,
Hold Infinity[1] in the palm[2] of your hand,
And Eternity[3] in an hour.

↗ William Blake (1757-1827) ✶

Comprehension

🍂 *What is the poet's message in this poem?*
a. We should hold on to an infinite amount of sand and wild flower
   in the palm of your hand for an hour.
b. Some small things are reflections of bigger things in life and
   anyone of us is capable of a lot.
c. We should make best use of time.

1. infinity [ɪn'fɪnɪti] (n.) a limitless amount, space, quantity or period of time, boundless or endless numbers 無限；無窮
2. palm [pɑːm] (n.) the inner side of a hand that is between the fingers and the wrist 手掌
3. eternity [ɪ'tɜːrnəti] (n.) an endless period of time 永恆

Winged Figure (Abbott Handerson Thayer, 1849-1921)

51 | I Wandered Lonely As a Cloud

I wandered[1] lonely as a cloud
That floats on high o'er vales[2] and hills,
When all at once I saw a crowd[3],
A host, of golden daffodils[4];
Beside the lake beneath[5] the trees,
Fluttering[6] and dancing in the breeze.

↗ William Wordsworth (1770-1850):
I Wandered Lonely as a Cloud *

Comprehension

🍁 *In this poem, Wordsworth used some words of contrast to express his feelings. What are they?*

🍁 *What was Wordsworth trying to tell us through this poem?*

1. wander ['wɑːndər] (v.) to move around without a specific destination nor a fixed course, aim, or goal 漫步；徘徊
2. vale [veɪl] (n.) a valley 山谷
3. crowd [kraʊd] (n.) a large number of people or things gathered together 人群
4. daffodil ['dæfədɪl] (n.) any of various plants (genus Narcissus) of the lily family with a typically yellow flower with a trumpet-shaped central corona 黃水仙
5. beneath [bɪ'niːθ] (prep.) directly under 在下方
6. flutter ['flʌtər] (v.) to move with quick wavering or flapping motions, to vibrate rapidly and irregularly 振翼；拍翅

52 Nature

🎧 52

There is a pleasure in the pathless woods,
There is a rapture[1] on the lonely shore,
There is society, where none intrudes[2],
By the deep sea, and music in its roar:
I love not man the less, but Nature more,
From these our interviews, in which I steal
From all I may be, or have been before,
To mingle[3] with the Universe, and feel
What I can ne'er[4] express, yet connot[5] all conceal[6].

↗ George Gordon Byron (1788-1824):
Childe Harold's Pilgrimage ✶

Comprehension

🍁 *How did Byron feel about man and society?*
🍁 *How did Byron feel about nature?*

1. rapture ['ræptʃər] (n.) the state of an overwhelming emotion, usually of ecstasy or passion 狂喜
2. intrude [ɪn'truːd] (v.) to force in inappropriately without permission or invitation 侵入
3. mingle ['mɪŋɡəl] (v.) to bring or mix together 混合；融入
4. ne'er (adv.) contraction of "never" 「never」的縮寫
5. connot (aux.) old English for "cannot" 「cannot」的古英文用法
6. conceal [kən'siːl] (v.) to keep from being seen or found 隱藏

Saint Genevieve (Charles Sprague Pearce, 1851-1914)

53 Happiness

There is that in me—I do not know what it is—but I know it
is in me.
Wrench[1]'d and sweaty[2]—calm and cool then my body
becomes.
I sleep—I sleep long.
I do not know it—it is without name—it is a word unsaid,
It is not in any dictionary, utterance[3], symbol[4] . . .
Do you see O my brothers and sisters?
It is not chaos[5] or death—it is form, union, plan—it is
eternal[6] life—it is Happiness.

↗ Walt Whitman (1819-1892):
Leaves of Grass ⋆

Comprehension

🍃 *What are some words of contrasts used by Whitman in this poem?*

🍁 *Summarize Whitman's definition of "happiness."*

1. wrench [rentʃ] (v.) to be twisted or pulled violently 用力扭轉
2. sweaty ['swɛti] (a.) covered with sweat 汗濕的
3. utterance ['ʌtərəns] (n.) vocal expression 話語；言詞
4. symbol ['sɪmbəl] (n.) something that stands for or suggests something
   else by reason of relationship, association, convention, or accidental
   resemblance 象徵；符號
5. chaos ['keɪɑːs] (n.) a state of confusion or disorder 失序；混沌
6. eternal [ɪ'tɜːrnəl] (a.) having infinite duration, without end 永恆的

Proserpine (Dante Gabriel Rossetti, 1828-1882)

54 If I Can Stop One Heart From Breaking

If I can stop one heart from breaking,
I shall not live in vain[1];
If I can ease[2] one life the aching,
Or cool one pain,
Or help one fainting[3] robin[4]
Unto his nest again
I shall not live in vain.

↗ Emily Dickinson (1830-1886) ✲

Comprehension

🍁 *What did Emily Dickinson think were the purposes of her life?*
🍂 *Through this poem, can you describe what kind of person Dickinson might be?*

1. in vain: without success or result 無用；徒勞
2. ease [iːz] (v.) to reduce the level of discomfort or pain 減輕；緩和
3. faint [feɪnt] (v.) to lose consciousness because of a temporary decrease in the blood supply to the brain 昏厥
4. robin ['rɑːbɪn] (n.) a North American thrush having grayish back, blackish head and tail, black and whitish streaked throat, and dull reddish breast and belly 知更鳥

The Birthday Party (John Singer Sargent, 1856-1925)

55 A Birthday Poem (for Rachel)

55

For every year of life we light
A candle on your cake
To mark the simple sort of progress
Anyone can make,
And then, to test your nerve[1] or give
A proper view of death,
You're asked to blow each light, each year,
Out with your own breath.

↗ James Simmons (1933–2001) ✲

Comprehension

❧ *What do the candles represent in this poem?*
❧ *What are some examples of progress referred to in this poem?*
❧ *What does it mean to blow out each candle?*

1. nerve [nɜːrv] (n.) daringness 膽量

The Sense of Sight
(Annie Louise Swynnerton, 1844-1933)

56 Dreams

Hold fast[1] to dreams
For if dreams die
Life is a broken-winged bird
That cannot fly.
Hold fast to dreams
For when dreams go
Life is a barren[2] field
Frozen with snow.

↗ Langston Hughes (1902-1967) ☀

Comprehension

🍁 *According to Langston Hughes, what gives life meaning?*

1. fast [fæst] (adv.) allowing no movement or no chance of slipping or escape 緊地；牢固地
2. barren ['bærən] (a.) unproductive, producing little or no vegetation 貧瘠的

57 Who Has Seen the Wind?

Who has seen the wind?
Neither I nor you;
But when the leaves hang trembling
The wind is passing through.

Who has seen the wind?
Neither you nor I;
But when the trees bow down their heads
The wind is passing by.

↗ Christina Rossetti (1830-1894) ✶

Comprehension

❧ *What was the message that the poet wanted to convey?*
  *a. Trees are like people because they tremble and they have heads
     too.*
  b. Trees move because of the wind.
  *c. Even though there are some things that we can't see with our
     eyes, they may still have an effect on us.*

58 The Daisies

In the scented bud of the morning—O,
When the windy grass went rippling[1] far,
I saw my dear one walking slow,
In the fields where the daisies[2] are.

We did not laugh and we did not speak
As we wandered happily to and fro[3];
I kissed my dear on either cheek,
In the bud of the morning—O.

A lark[4] sang up from the breezy land,
A lark sang down from a cloud afar[5],
And she and I went hand in hand
In the field where the daisies are.

↗ James Stephens (1882-1950) ☆

Comprehension

🍁 *In this poem, what was probably the relationship of the poet to his "dear?"*

🍁 *What writing techniques did James Stephens use in this poem?*
   a. metaphor b. analogy c. parallelism d. contrast

1. ripple ['rɪpəl] (v.) to form a series of small waves on the surface 起漣漪
2. daisy ['deɪzi] (n.) a plant of the composite family, bearing flowers with white rays around a yellow disk 雛菊
3. fro [froʊ] (adv.) old English for "back," now only used in the phrase of "to and fro" 「back」的古英文用法，如今只出現在「to and fro」這個片語裡
4. lark [lɑːrk] (n.) a kind of small songbird that are usually brownish in color, especially skylark 雲雀
5. afar [ə'fɑːr] (adv.) from, to, or at a distance 遠方；遙遠地

Caecilia met de harp (Antoon van Welie, 1866-1956)

59 To—

Music, when soft voices die,
Vibrates in the memory—
Odors, when sweet violets sicken,
Live within the sense they quicken.
Rose leaves, when the rose is dead,
Are heaped for the beloved's bed;
And so thy[1] thoughts, when thou art[2] gone,
Love itself shall slumber[3] on.

↗ Percy Bysshe Shelley (1792-1822) ✳

Comprehension

🍁 *According to the poem, what are the four things that will remain*
after their sources die?

1. thy [ðaɪ] (pron.) old English for "your" 古英語的「your」
2. art [ɑːrt] (aux.) old English for "are" 古英語的「are」(第二人稱單數 be
   動詞)
3. slumber ['slʌmbər] (v.) to sleep lightly 睡眠；微睡

Ulysses and the Sirens (John William Waterhouse, 1849-1917)

60 The Love Song of J. Alfred Prufrock

🎧 60 I grow old . . . I grow old . . .
I shall wear the bottoms of my trousers rolled.

Shall I part my hair behind? Do I dare to eat a peach?
I shall wear white flannel[1] trousers, and walk upon the
  beach.
I have heard the mermaids singing, each to each.

I do not think that they will sing to me.

I have seen them riding seaward on the waves
Combing the white hair of the waves blown back
When the wind blows the water white and black.

We have lingered in the chambers[2] of the sea
By sea-girls wreathed with seaweed red and brown
Till human voices wake us, and we drown.

↗ T.S. Eliot (1888-1965) ☆

---

1. flannel ['flænl] (n.) a soft light woolen fabric 法蘭絨
2. chamber ['tʃeɪmbər] (n.) a natural or artificial enclosed space 室；房間

Part 2__
Reading Moments

Part 2

1 Speeches & Countries

Declaration of Independence (John Trumbull, 1756-1843)

61 Declaration of Independence

We hold these truths to be self-evident, that all men are created equal, that they are endowed[1] by their Creator with certain unalienable[2] rights, that among these are life, liberty, and the pursuit of happiness.

That, to secure these rights, governments are instituted among men, deriving their just powers from the consent of the governed.

That, whenever any form of government becomes destructive of these ends, it is the right of the people to alter[3] or to abolish[4] it, and to institute[5] new government, laying its foundation on such principles, and organizing its powers in such form, as to them shall seem most likely to effect their safety and happiness.

↗ Thomas Jefferson (1743-1826)

---

1. endow [ɪnˈdaʊ] (v.) to give qualities or abilities to 賦予
2. unalienable [ʌnˈeɪliənəbl] (a.) something that cannot be taken away from you 不可剝奪的
3. alter [ˈɔːltər] (v.) to change something, usually slightly, or to cause the characteristics of something to change 改變
4. abolish [əˈbɑːlɪʃ] (v.) to officially end a law, system etc, especially one that has existed for a long time 廢除
5. institute [ˈɪnstətuːt] (v.) to set up or lay the groundwork for 創建

THESE DEAD . . . SHALL N⊕T HAVE DIED IN VAIN.

"You have a greater task than I had.

Slavery must be removed from the whole of the earth."

62 The Four Freedoms

In the future days, which we seek to make secure, we look forward to a world founded upon four essential human freedoms.

The first is freedom of speech and expression everywhere in the world.

The second is freedom of every person to worship God in his own way everywhere in the world.

The third is freedom from want, which, translated into world terms, means economic understandings which will secure to every nation a healthy peacetime life for its inhabitants everywhere in the world.

The fourth is freedom from fear—which, translated into world terms, means a worldwide reduction of armaments[1] to such a point and in such a thorough fashion that no nation will be in a position to commit an act of physical aggression against any neighbor—anywhere in the world.

↗ Franklin D. Roosevelt (1882-1945):
January 6, 1941, one of annual messages to Congress

1. armaments ['ɑːrməmənts] (n.) (pl.) weaponry used by military or naval force 軍備

A Flower for the Teacher
(Winslow Homer, 1836-1910)

63 American Dream

63 I say to you today, my friends, that in spite of the difficulties and frustrations[1] of the moment I still have a dream. It is a dream deeply rooted in the American dream[2].

I have a dream that one day this nation will rise up and live out the true meaning of its creed[3]: "We hold these truths to be self-evident, that all men are created equal."

I have a dream that one day on the red hills of Georgia, sons of former slaves and sons of former slave-owners will be able to sit down together at the table of brotherhood.

I have a dream that one day, even the state of Mississippi, a state sweltering[4] with the heat of injustice and oppression[5], will be transformed into an oasis of freedom and justice.

I have a dream my four little children will one day live in a nation where they will not be judged by the color of their skin but by content of their character. I have a dream today!

1. frustration [frʌ'streɪʃən] (n.) a feeling of annoyance at being hindered or criticized 挫折
2. American dream: the widespread aspiration of Americans to live better than their parents did 美國夢 (指追求自由、機會均等、富庶等)
3. creed [kriːd] (n.) a set of beliefs which expresses a particular opinion and influences the way you live 信念；綱領
4. swelter ['sweltər] (v.) to be very hot in a way that makes you feel uncomfortable 熱得難受；熱得發昏
5. oppression [ə'preʃən] (n.) when someone treats a group of people unfairly or cruelly and prevents them from having the same rights as other people have 壓迫

Injustice anywhere is a threat to justice everywhere.
Dr. Martin Luther King Jr.

Hartshorn '07

I have a dream that one day the state of Alabama, whose governor's lips are presently dripping[6] with the words of interposition[7] and nullification[8], will be transformed into a situation where little black boys and black girls will be able to join hands with little white boys and white girls and walk together as sisters and brothers. I have a dream today!

I have a dream that one day every valley shall be exalted[9], every hill and mountain shall be made low, rough places will be made plains, and the crooked[10] places will be made straight, and the glory of the Lord shall be revealed, and all flesh[11] shall see it together.

This is our hope. This is the faith with which I return to the South. With this faith we will be able to hew[12] out of the mountain of despair a stone of hope. With this faith we will be able to transform the jangling[13] discords[14] of our nation into a beautiful symphony[15] of brotherhood. With this faith we will be able to work together, to pray together, to struggle together, to go to jail together, to stand up for freedom together, knowing that we will be free one day.

↗ Martin Luther King (1929-1968): *I Have a Dream*

6. drip [drɪp] (v.) to contain or be covered in a lot of something
   充溢；充滿
7. interposition [ˌɪntərpəˈzɪʃən] (n.) the action of interjecting or interposing an action or remark that interrupts 介入；干預
8. nullification [ˌnʌlɪfɪˈkeɪʃən] (n.) cancellation of something 廢除；取消
9. exalt [ɪɡˈzɑːlt] (v.) to put someone or something into a high rank or position 使升高
10. crooked [ˈkrʊkɪd] (a.) not forming a straight line; having many sharp bends 彎曲的；變形的
11. flesh [fleʃ] (n.) human beings（不可數）眾生
12. hew [hjuː] (v.) to cut something with a cutting tool 劈出；開闢
13. jangling [ˈdʒæŋɡəlɪŋ] (a.) like the discordant ringing of nonmusical metallic objects striking together 發出不和諧刺耳聲的
14. discord [ˈdɪskɔːrd] (n.) a group of musical notes which give an unpleasant sound when played together 噪音；喧鬧
15. symphony [ˈsɪmfəni] (n.) a long complicated piece of music for a large orchestra 交響樂；交響曲

64 Inaugural Address

64   In the long history of the world, only a few generations have been granted the role of defending[1] freedom in its hour of maximum danger.

I do not shrink[2] from this responsibility—I welcome it. I do not believe that any of us would exchange places with any other people or any other generation. The energy, the faith, the devotion which we bring to this endeavor[3] will light our country and all who serve it—and the glow from that fire can truly light the world.

And so, my fellow Americans: Ask not what your country can do for you—ask what you can do for your country.

My fellow citizens of the world: Ask not what America will do for you, but what together we can do for the freedom of man.

Finally, whether you are citizens of America or citizens of the world, ask of us here the same high standards of strength and sacrifice which we ask of you. With a good conscience[4] which we ask of you, with a good conscience our only sure reward, with history the final judge of our deeds, let us go forth to lead the land we love, asking His blessing and His help, but knowing that here on earth God's work must truly be our own.

↗ John Fitzgerald Kennedy (1917-1963)

---

1. defend [dɪˈfɛnd] (v.) to protect somebody or something from attack, harm, or danger 保衛
2. shrink [ʃrɪŋk] (v.) to move back or away from something because you are frightened or shocked 回避；退避
3. endeavor [ɪnˈdɛvər] (n.) an effort or attempt 努力
4. conscience [ˈkɑːnʃəns] (n.) the part of your mind that tells you whether what you are doing is morally right or wrong 良心；善惡觀念

65 I Hear America Singing

 I hear America singing, the varied carols[1] I hear,
Those of mechanics[2], each one singing his
as it should blithe[3] and strong,
The carpenter singing his
as he measures his plank[4] or beam[5],
The mason[6] singing his as he makes ready for work,
or leaves off[7] work,
The boatman singing what belongs to him in his boat,
the deck-hand[8] singing on the steamboat deck,
The shoemaker singing as he sits on his bench,
the hatter[9] singing as he stands,

The woodcutter's song,
the plowboy's[10] on his way in the morning,
or at noon intermission[11] or a sundown[12],
The delicious singing of the mother,
or of the young wife at work,
or of the girl sewing or washing,
Each singing what belongs to him or her
and to none else,
The day what belongs to the day—
at night the party of young fellows, robust[13],
friendly,
Singing with open mouths their strong melodious
songs.

↗ Walt Whitman (1819-1892): *Leaves of Grass*

1. carol ['kærəl] (n.) a happy or religious song, usually one sung at Christmas（耶誕）頌歌；讚美詩
2. mechanics [mɪ'kænɪks] (n.) the branch of physics concerned with the motion of bodies in a frame of reference 機械學
3. blithe [blaɪð] (a.) happy, cheerful, and carefree 歡樂的；快活的
4. plank [plæŋk] (n.) a long, flat piece of lumber sawn thicker than a board 木板（條）；厚板
5. beam [biːm] (n.) a long thick piece of wood, metal or concrete, especially used to support weight in a building or other structure 梁；桁
6. mason ['meɪsən] (n.) somebody who works with stone or brick, especially in the building trades 石匠；水泥匠
7. leave off: to stop, or to stop doing something 停止
8. deck-hand ['dekhænd] (n.) a member of a ship's crew who performs manual labor 甲板水手；一般水手
9. hatter ['hætər] (n.) a maker or seller of hats 帽商
10. plowboy ['plaʊbɔɪ] (n.) a boy who leads or guides a team of animals in plowing 農家子弟
11. intermission [ɪntə'mɪʃən] (n.) a time interval during which there is a temporary cessation of something 間歇；暫停
12. sundown ['sʌndaʊn] (n.) the time when the Sun sets 日落
13. robust [rə'bʌst] (a.) strong, healthy, and hardy in constitution 強健的；結實的

66 New York

🎧66 A poem compresses[1] much in a small space and adds music, thus heightening its meaning. The city is like poetry: it compresses all life, all races and breeds[2], into a small island and adds music and accompaniment[3] of internal engines. The island of Manhattan is without any doubt the greatest human concentrate[4] on earth, the poem whose magic is comprehensible to millions of permanent residents but whose full meaning will always remain illusive[5].

At the feet of the tallest and plushiest[6] offices lie the crummiest[7] slums[8]. The genteel[9] mysteries housed in the Riverside Church are only a few blocks from the voodoo[10] charms[11] of Harlem[12]. The merchant princes, riding to Wall Street in their limousines[13] down the East River Drive, pass within a few hundred yards of the gypsy kings; but the princes do not know they are passing the kings, and the kings are not up yet anyway—they live a more leisurely[14] life than the princes and get drunk more consistently.

↗ E. B. White (1899-1985):
Here Is New York

1. compress ['kɑːmprɛs] (v.) to press something into a smaller space 壓縮
2. breed [briːd] (n.) a type of person 種類；類型
3. accompaniment [ə'kʌmpənimənt] (n.) a subordinate musical part 〔音〕伴奏；伴唱
4. concentrate ['kɑːnsəntreɪt] (n.) a substance or liquid which has been made stronger by removing most of the water from it 濃縮物
5. illusive [ɪ'luːsɪv] (a.) based on or having the nature of an illusion, an idea or belief which is not true 夢幻似的；迷惑人的
6. plush [plʌʃ] (a.) luxurious, expensive, or lavish 〔口〕豪華的；奢侈的
7. crummy ['krʌmi] (a.) of very bad quality 骯髒的；破舊的；寒酸的
8. slum [slʌm] (n.) an overcrowded area of a city in which the housing is typically in very bad condition 貧民窟；陋巷
9. genteel [dʒen'tiːl] (a.) quiet and polite, often in an exaggerated way 〔文〕彬彬有禮的；附庸風雅的
10. voodoo ['vuːduː] (n.) magical beliefs and practices used as a form of religion, especially by people in Haiti 巫毒教
11. charm [tʃɑːrm] (n.) an object or saying which is thought to possess magical powers, such as the ability to bring good luck 符咒；護身符
12. Harlem ['hɑːrləm] (n.) district of Manhattan; now largely a Black ghetto 哈林區（美國紐約市黑人區）
13. limousine ['lɪməziːn] (n.) a large luxurious car 大型豪華轎車；大轎車
14. leisurely ['liːʒərli] (adv.) done without hurrying 從容不迫地

67 Nostalgia

🎧 67 It is a curious emotion, this certain homesickness I have in mind. With Americans, it is a national trait[1], as native to us as the roller coaster[2] or the jukebox[3]. It is no simple longing for the home town or country of our birth. The emotion is Janusfaced[4]: we are torn between a nostalgia[5] for the familiar and an urge for the foreign and strange. As often as not, we are homesick most for the places we have never known.

↗ Carson McCullers (1917-1967):
Look Homeward, Americans

1. trait [treɪt] (n.) a particular characteristic that can produce a particular type of behavior 特徵
2. roller coaster: an amusement park ride consisting of a narrow rail track on a metal framework shaped into extreme peaks and troughs and sharp bends 雲霄飛車
3. jukebox [ˈdʒuːkbɑːks] (n.) a machine in bars etc. which plays recorded music when a coin is put into it 投幣式自動點唱機
4. janusfaced [ˈdʒeɪnəsfeɪst] (a.) having two contrasting aspects, as the alternation of mood in a capricious person 有兩副面孔的
5. nostalgia [nɑːˈstældʒə] (n.) a mixed feeling of happiness, sadness, and longing when recalling a person, place, or event from the past, or the past in general 鄉愁；懷舊情懷

68 England and the English

There is nothing so bad or so good that you will not find an Englishman doing it; but you will never find an Englishman in the wrong. He does everything on principle. He fights you on patriotic[1] principles; he robs you on business principles; he enslaves[2] you on imperial[3] principles; he bullies[4] you on manly principles; he supports his king on loyal principles and cuts off his king's head on republican principles. His watchword[5] is always Duty; and he never forgets that the nation which lets its duty get on the opposite side to its interest is lost.

↗ George Bernard Shaw (1856-1950):
The Man of Destiny

1. patriotic [ˌpeɪtriˈɑːtɪk] (a.) showing love for your country and pride in it 愛國的
2. enslave [ɪnˈsleɪv] (v.) to take somebody prisoner and claim legal ownership of that person and his or her labor 奴役
3. imperial [ɪmˈpɪriəl] (a.) involving or relating to the authority of a country over colonies or other countries 最高權力的；專橫的
4. bully [ˈbʊli] (v.) to hurt or frighten someone who is smaller or less powerful than you, often forcing them to do something they do not want to do 霸凌；威嚇；欺侮
5. watchword [ˈwɑːtʃwɜːrd] (n.) a word or slogan that encapsulates a mode of action, a set of beliefs, or membership of a group 口號；標語

London: Westminster Abbey,
With a Procession of Knights of the Bath (Canaletto, 1697-1768)

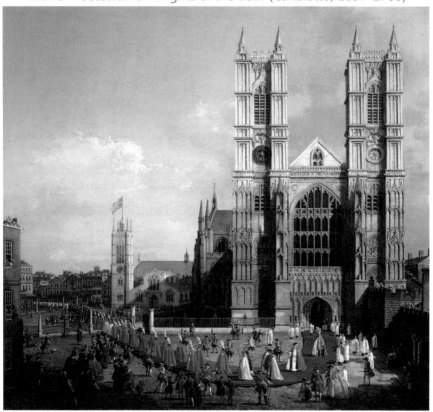

69 Westminster Abbey

When I look upon the tombs of the great, every emotion of envy dies in me; when I read the epitaphs[1] of the beautiful, every inordinate[2] desire goes out; when I meet with the grief of parents upon a tombstone, my heart melts with compassion; when I see the tomb of the parents themselves, I consider the vanity[3] of grieving for those whom we must quickly follow; when I see kings lying by those who deposed[4] them, when I consider rival wits placed side by side, or the holy men that divided the world with their contests and disputes[5], I reflect with sorrow and astonishment on the little competitions, factions[6], and debates of mankind. When I read the several dates of the tombs, of some that dies yesterday, and some six hundred years ago, I consider that great Day when we shall all of us be contemporaries, and make our appearance together.

↗ Joseph Addison (1672-1719):
Spectator (No. 26)

1. epitaph ['ɛpɪtæf] (n.) an inscription on a tombstone or monument commemorating the person buried there 墓誌銘；碑文
2. inordinate [ɪ'nɔːrdənɪt] (a.) exceeding reasonable limits; immoderate 過度的；放縱的
3. vanity ['vænəti] (n.) the state or fact of being futile, worthless, or empty of significance 無意義
4. depose [dɪ'poʊz] (v.) to remove someone important from a powerful position 罷免；廢（王位）
5. dispute [dɪ'spjuːt] (n.) a serious argument or disagreement 爭論；爭執
6. faction ['fækʃən] (n.) conflict within an organization or nation; internal dissension 內訌

Louis XVI (1754-1793),
King of France

70 French Revolution

It was the best of times, it was the worst of times, it was the age of wisdom, it was the age of foolishness, it was the epoch of belief, it was the epoch[1] of incredulity[2], it was the season of Light, it was the season of Darkness, it was the spring of hope, it was the winter of despair, we had everything before us, we had nothing before us, we were all going direct to Heaven, we were all going direct the other way—in short, the period was so far like the present period, that some of its noisiest authorities insisted on its being received, for good or for evil, in the superlative[3] degree of comparison only.

↗ Charles Dickens (1818-1870):
A Tale of Two Cities

1. epoch ['ɛpək] (n.) a significant period in history or in somebody's life
   時期；時代
2. incredulity [ˌɪnkrɪ'duːlɪti] (n.) the state or quality of being incredulous;
   disbelief 懷疑
3. superlative [sʊ'pɜːrlətɪv] (a.) of the highest quality; the best
   過度的；誇大的

Napoleon Crossing the Alps (Jacques-Louis David, 1748-1825)

71 | The Battle of Waterloo

🎧 71 ▸ All that day, from morning until past sunset, the cannon never ceased to roar. It was dark when the cannonading[1] stopped all of a sudden.

All of us have read of what occurred during that interval. The tale is in every Englishman's mouth; and you and I, who were children when the great battle was won and lost, are never tired of hearing and recounting the history of that famous action.

Its remembrance rankles[2] still in the bosoms[3] of millions of the countrymen of those brave men who lost the day. They pant[4] for an opportunity of revenging that humiliation[5]; and if a contest, ending in a victory on their part, should ensue[6], elating[7] them in their turn, and leaving its cursed legacy[8] of hatred and rage behind to us, there is no end to the so-called glory and shame, and to the alternations of successful and unsuccessful murder, in which two high-spirited nations might engage.

Centuries hence, we Frenchmen and Englishmen might be boasting and killing each other still, carrying out bravely the Devil's code of honor.

↗ William Makepeace Thackeray (1811-1863):
Vanity Fair

Napoleon I on His Imperial Throne
(Jean Auguste Dominique Ingres, 1780-1867)

1. cannonade [ˌkænəˈneɪd] (n.) a period of continuous heavy firing of large guns, especially as part of an attack（連續）炮擊；炮轟
2. rankle [ˈræŋkəl] (v.) to cause persistent feelings of bitterness, resentment, or anger 仍令人怨恨難消
3. bosom [ˈbʊzəm] (n.) the place where emotions are felt 內心；胸懷
4. pant [pænt] (v.) to want someone or something very much 渴望
5. humiliation [hjuːˌmɪliˈeɪʃən] (n.) the feeling or condition of being lessened in dignity or pride 羞辱
6. ensue [ɪnˈsuː] (v.) to happen after something else, especially as a result of it〔書〕接著發生
7. elate [ɪˈleɪt] (v.) to make somebody very happy and excited 使興奮；使得意
8. legacy [ˈlegəsi] (n.) something that is handed down or remains from a previous generation or time 留給後人的東西；遺產

2 Biographies

Walt Whitman (1819-1892)

72 Walt Whitman

In his very rejection[1] of art Walt Whitman is an artist. He tried to produce a certain effect by certain means and he succeeded . . . He stands apart, and the chief value of his work is in its prophecy[2], not in its performance. He has begun a prelude[3] to larger themes. He is the herald[4] to a new era. As man he is the precursor[5] of a fresh type. He is a factor[6] in the heroic and spiritual evolution of the human being. If Poetry has passed him by, Philosophy will take note of him.

↗ Oscar Wilde (1854-1900):
Review of Whitman

1. rejection [rɪˈdʒekʃən] (n.) when someone refuses to accept, use or believe someone or something 拒絕；摒棄
2. prophecy [ˈprɑːfɪsi] (n.) a prediction that something will occur in the future 預言
3. prelude [ˈpreljuːd] (n.) an event or action that introduces or precedes something else, especially something longer and more important 前奏；序幕
4. herald [ˈherəld] (n.) an official messenger and representative of a king or leader in former times 傳令官；預報者
5. precursor [prɪˈkɜːrsər] (n.) somebody or something that comes before, and is often considered to lead to the development of, another person or thing 先驅
6. factor [ˈfæktər] (n.) a fact or situation which influences the result of something 因素；要素

73 William Shakespeare

73 We become lovers when we see Romeo and Juliet, and Hamlet makes us students. The blood of Duncan[1] is upon our hands, with Timon[2] we rage[3] against the world, and when Lear[4] wanders out upon the heath[5] the terror of madness touches us. Ours is the white sinlessness of Desdemona[6], and ours, also, the sin of Iago[7].

↗ Oscar Wilde (1854-1900):
The Portrait of Mr. W. H.

1. Duncan : one of the characters of William Shakespeare's play *Macbeth* 出自莎士比亞四大悲劇之一的 Macbeth（馬克白），Duncan 在劇中為蘇格蘭國王，後遭馬克白暗殺。
2. Timon : the main character of *Timon of Athens* by William Shakespeare 出自莎士比亞的 Timon of Athens，Timon 即劇中主人翁。
3. rage [reɪdʒ] (v.) to speak or do something with sudden, extreme anger, or feel such strong anger 發怒
4. Lear: one of the main characters of William Shakespeare's play *King Lear* 出自莎士比亞四大悲劇之一的 King Lear（李爾王），李爾後來因兒女的不孝與虐待而發瘋。
5. heath [hiːθ] (n.) an area of land that is not farmed, where grass and other small plants grow, but where there are few trees or bushes（長石南植物的）荒原
6. Desdemona: a character in Shakespeare's *Othello*; Othello's wife 出自莎士比亞四大悲劇之一的 Othello（奧瑟羅），為主人翁奧瑟羅之妻，後來成為奧瑟羅嫉妒之心下的無辜犧牲品。
7. Iago: a fictional character in Shakespeare's *Othello*; a trusted advisor to Othello but mislead Othello into believing that Desdemona is having an affair with one of his chief lieutenants 出自莎士比亞四大悲劇之一的 Othello（奧瑟羅），陰險設計奧瑟羅對妻子 Desdemona 產生疑心。

74 Three Passions

Three passions, simple but overwhelmingly strong, have governed my life: the longing for love, the search for knowledge, and unbearable pity for the suffering of mankind. These passions, like great winds, have blown me hither and thither, in a wayward[1] course, over a deep ocean of anguish[2], reaching to the very verge[3] of despair.

I have sought love, first, because it brings ecstasy[4]—ecstasy so great that I would often have sacrificed all the rest of life for a few hours of this joy. I have sought it, next, because it relieves loneliness—that terrible loneliness in which one shivering[5] consciousness looks over the rim[6] of the world into the cold unfathomable[7] lifeless abyss[8]. I have sought it, finally, because in the union of love I have seen, in a mystic miniature[9], the prefiguring[10] vision of the heaven that saints and poets have imagined. This is what I sought, and though it might seem too good for human life, this is what—at last—I have found.

With equal passion I have sought knowledge. I have wished to understand the hearts of men. I have wished to know why the stars shine. And I have tried to apprehend the Pythagorean power by which number holds sway[11] above the flux[12]. A little of this, but not much, I have achieved.

Love and knowledge, so far as they were possible, led upward toward the heavens. But always pity brought me back to earth. Echoes of cries of pain reverberate[13] in my heart. Children in famine[14], victims tortured by oppressors[15], helpless old people a hated burden to their sons, and the whole world of loneliness, poverty, and pain make a mockery[16] of what human life should be. I long to alleviate[17] the evil, but I cannot, and I too suffer.

This has been my life. I have found it worth living, and would gladly live it again if the chance were offered me.

↗ Bertrand Russell (1872-1970):
Autobiography

1. wayward [ˈweɪwərd] (a.) changeable, selfish, and difficult to control 難捉摸的；不規則的
2. anguish [ˈæŋgwɪʃ] (n.) extreme anxiety or emotional torment 極度的痛苦；苦惱
3. verge [vɜːrdʒ] (n.) the edge or border of something 邊緣
4. ecstasy [ˈekstəsi] (n.) a state of extreme happiness, especially when feeling pleasure 狂喜；出神；入迷
5. shivering [ˈʃɪvərɪŋ] (a.) (with fear or cold) vibrating slightly and irregularly 顫抖的；使顫抖的
6. rim [rɪm] (n.) an outer edge, often slightly raised, that runs along the outside of something curved or circular 邊；緣
7. unfathomable [ʌnˈfæðəməbəl] (a.) impossible to understand 深不可測的
8. abyss [əˈbɪs] (n.) a very deep hole which seems to have no bottom 深淵
9. miniature [ˈmɪniətʃər] (n.) a smaller-than-usual version of something 縮樣；縮圖
10. prefigure [ˌpriːˈfɪgjər] (v.) to think about or imagine a person, thing, or event in advance 預示；預想
11. sway [sweɪ] (n.) control or influence 支配；統治
12. flux [flʌks] (n.) constant change and instability 變遷
13. reverberate [rɪˈvɜːrbəreɪt] (v.) to echo repeatedly（使）迴響
14. famine [ˈfæmɪn] (n.) a severe shortage of food resulting in widespread hunger 饑荒；饑餓
15. oppressor [əˈpresər] (n.) someone who treats people in an unfair and cruel way and prevents them from having opportunities and freedom 壓迫者
16. mockery [ˈmɑːkəri] (n.) words or behavior intended to make somebody or something look silly or ridiculous 嘲笑；嘲弄
17. alleviate [əˈliːvieɪt] (v.) to make something bad such as pain or problems less severe 減輕；緩和

Jack London (1876-1916)

75 Life Worth Living

 I was born in the working-class. Early I discovered enthusiasm, ambition, and ideals; and to satisfy these became the problem of my child-life. My environment was crude[1] and rough and raw. I had no outlook[2], but an uplook rather. My place in society was at the bottom. Here life offered nothing but sordidness[3] and wretchedness[4], both of the flesh and the spirit; for here flesh and spirit were alike starved and tormented[5].

Above me towered the colossal[6] edifice[7] of society, and to my mind the only way out was up. Into this edifice I early resolved to climb. Up above, men wore black clothes and boiled shirts[8], and women dressed in beautiful gowns[9]. Also, there were good things to eat, and there was plenty to eat. This much for the flesh. Then there were the things of the spirit.

Up above me, I knew, were unselfishnesses of the spirit, clean and noble thinking, keen intellectual living. I knew all this because I read "Seaside Library" novels, in which, with the exception of the villains[10] and adventuresses, all men and women thought beautiful thoughts, spoke a beautiful tongue, and performed glorious deeds. In short, as I accepted the rising of the sun, I accepted that up above me was all that was fine and noble and gracious, all that gave decency[11] and dignity[12] to life, all that made life worth living and that remunerated[13] one for his travail[14] and misery.

↗ Jack London (1876-1916):
What Life Means to Me

1. crude [kruːd] (a.) in a rough or incomplete state 粗野的；粗糙的
2. outlook ['aʊtlʊk] (n.) expectations for the future, especially with respect to a particular situation 展望；前景
3. sordidness ['sɔːrdɪdnəs] (n.) the quality or state of being dirty and unpleasant 骯髒；卑下
4. wretchedness ['retʃɪdnəs] (n.) a state of ill-being due to affliction or misfortune 悲慘；痛苦
5. torment ['tɔːrment] (v.) to inflict torture, pain, or anguish on a person or animal 使痛苦；折磨
6. colossal [kə'lɑːsəl] (a.) extremely large 〔口〕驚人的；可觀的
7. edifice ['edɪfɪs] (n.) a large building, especially a splendid one 大廈；雄偉的建築物
8. boiled shirt: a formal or semiformal dress shirt with a starched front 禮服襯衫；〔美俚〕漿過硬挺的襯衫
9. gown [gaʊn] (n.) a woman's full-length elegant or formal dress for special occasions 女禮服
10. villain ['vɪlən] (n.) an evil character in a novel, movie, play, or other story, especially one who is the main enemy of the hero 壞人；惡棍
11. decency ['diːsənsi] (n.) behavior that is good, moral and acceptable in society 正派；高雅；端莊
12. dignity ['dɪgnəti] (n.) a proper sense of pride and self-respect 尊嚴；莊嚴
13. remunerate [rɪ'mjuːnəreɪt] (v.) to pay somebody for goods or services, or compensate somebody financially for losses sustained or inconvenience caused 賠償；給……酬勞
14. travail ['træveɪl] (n.) work, especially work that involves hard physical effort over a long period 痛苦；艱難

Edward Gibbon (1737-1794)

76 Past Love

🎧 76 I need not blush at recollecting the object of my choice; and though my love was disappointed of success, I am rather proud that I was once capable of feeling such a pure and exalted[1] sentiment[2]. The personal attractions of Mademoiselle Susan Curchod were embellished[3] by the virtues and talents of the mind . . .

The report of such a prodigy[4] awakened my curiosity: I saw and loved . . .

After a painful struggle I yielded to my fate: I sighed as a lover, I obeyed as a son; my wound was insensibly[5] healed by time, absence, and the habits of a new life. My cure was accelerated[6] by a faithful report of the tranquility[7] and cheerfulness of the lady herself, and my love subsided[8] in friendship and esteem.

↗ Edward Gibbon (1737-1794) :
Autobiography

---

1. exalted [ɪɡ'zɑːltd] (a.) in very high spirits 高貴的；崇高的
2. sentiment ['sentəmənt] (n.) gentle feelings such as sympathy, love, etc., especially when considered to be foolish or not suitable 感情；情操
3. embellish [ɪm'belɪʃ] (v.) to increase the beauty of something by adding ornaments or decorations 美化；裝飾
4. prodigy ['prɑːdɪdʒi] (n.) something very impressive or amazing 奇跡
5. insensibly [ɪn'sensɪbəlɪ] (adv.) in a numb manner; without feeling 不知不覺地
6. accelerate [ək'seləreɪt] (v.) to happen or make something happen sooner or faster 增長；增加
7. tranquility [træŋ'kwɪlɪti] (n.) a state of peace and calm 平靜
8. subside [səb'saɪd] (v.) to become less active or intense 平靜下來；平息

Mount Katahdin
(Frederic Edwin Church, 1826-1900)

77 Highest Reality

🎧 77   If the day and the night are such that you greet them with joy, and life emits[1] a fragrance[2] like flowers and sweet-scented herbs, is more elastic[3], more starry, more immortal—that is your success. All nature is your congratulation, and you have cause momentarily to bless yourself.

The greatest gains and values are farthest from being appreciated[4]. We easily come to doubt if they exist. We soon forget them. They are the highest reality. Perhaps the facts most astounding[5] and most real are never communicated by man to man.

The true harvest of my daily life is somewhat as intangible[6] and indescribable as the tints[7] of morning or evening. It is a little star-dust caught, a segment[8] of the rainbow which I have clutched[9].

↗ Henry D. Thoreau (1817-1862):

Walden

---

1. emit [ɪ'mɪt] (v.) to send out a beam, noise, smell or gas 散發；發出
2. fragrance ['freɪɡrəns] (n.) a pleasant sweet smell 芬芳；香味
3. elastic [ɪ'læstɪk] (a.) readily recovering from depression or exhaustion （心情）恢復的；開朗的
4. appreciate [ə'priːʃieɪt] (v.) to recognize or understand that something is valuable, important or as described 領會；察知
5. astounding [ə'staʊndɪŋ] (a.) very surprising or shocking 令人驚奇的
6. intangible [ɪn'tændʒɪbəl] (a.) lacking material qualities, and so not able to be touched or seen 觸摸不到的；無形的
7. tint [tɪnt] (n.) a small amount of a color 色彩；色調
8. segment ['seɡmənt] (n.) any of the parts into which something (especially a circle or sphere) can be divided or into which it is naturally divided 部分；斷片
9. clutch [klʌtʃ] (v.) to grip something tightly 抓住；攫取

Woman Walking in an Exotic Forest
(Henri Rousseau, 1844-1910)

78 Be Lost

🎧 78 🎧 In our most trivial[1] walks, we are constantly, though unconsciously, steering[2] like pilots by certain well-known beacons[3] and headlands[4], and if we go beyond our usual course we still carry in our minds the bearing[5] of some neighboring cape[6]; and not till we are completely lost, or turned round—for a man needs only to be turned round once with his eyes shut in this world to be lost—do we appreciate the vastness[7] and strangeness of nature. Every man has to learn the points of compass[8] again as often as be awaked, whether from sleep or any abstraction[9].

Not till we are lost, in other words not till we have lost the world, do we begin to find ourselves, and realize where we are and the infinite[10] extent of our relations.

↗ Henry D. Thoreau (1817-1862):
Walden

1. trivial ['trɪviəl] (a.) lacking any qualities that are unique or interesting 〔古〕普通的；平凡的
2. steer [stɪr] (v.) to control the direction of a vehicle 掌（船）舵
3. beacon ['biːkən] (n.) a lighthouse or signaling buoy that produces a flashing light to warn or guide ships 燈塔
4. headland ['hedlənd] (n.) a narrow piece of land jutting out into water, usually with steep high cliffs 〔地〕陸岬；海角
5. bearing ['berɪŋ] (n.) relevant relationship or interconnection 關係；關聯
6. cape [keɪp] (n.) a very large piece of land sticking out into the sea 岬；海角
7. vastness ['væstnəs] (n.) unusual largeness in size or extent or number 無邊無際；廣袤
8. compass ['kʌmpəs] (n.) a device for finding direction which has a freely moving needle that always points to magnetic north 羅盤；指南針
9. abstraction [æb'strækʃən] (n.) absence of mind 出神；心不在焉
10. infinite ['ɪnfɪnət] (a.) very great in size, number, degree, or extent 無限的；無窮的

79 Flints' Pond

Him who thought only of its money value; whose presence perchance cursed[1] all the shores; who exhausted[2] the land around it, and would fain have exhausted the waters within it; who regretted only that it was not English hay or cranberry[3] meadow—there was nothing to redeem[4] it, forsooth[5], in his eyes—and would have drained[6] and sold it for the mud at its bottom. It did not turn his mill, and it was no privilege[7] to him to behold it. I respect not his labors, his farm where everything has its price, who would carry the landscape, who would carry his God, to market, if he could get anything for him; who goes to market for his god as it is; on whose farm nothing grows free, whose fields bear[8] no crops, whose meadows no flowers, whose trees no fruits, but dollars; who loves not the beauty of his fruits, whose fruits are not ripe for him till they are turned to dollars.

↗ Henry D. Thoreau (1817-1862): *Walden*

1. curse [kɜːrs] (v.) to bring evil upon; afflict 使遭難
2. exhaust [ɪgˈzɔːst] (v.) to use up all that is available of something 耗盡；汲乾
3. cranberry [ˈkrænberi] (n.) a small round red fruit with a sour taste 蔓越橘；小紅莓
4. redeem [rɪˈdiːm] (v.) to make up for 補救；改善
5. forsooth [fərˈsuːθ] (adv.) in truth〔舊〕真的；的確
6. drain [dreɪn] (v.) to empty or dry something by allowing the water to flow out of or off it, or become empty or dry in this way 排掉（液體）；流出
7. privilege [ˈprɪvəlɪdʒ] (n.) the special right that some people in authority have which allows them to do or say things that other people are not allowed to （個人的）恩典；殊榮
8. bear [ber] (v.) to yield something by a natural process, or produce something desirable or valuable 生產（莊稼）

3 Essays

80 The Problem of Mankind

(Henri Martin, 1860-1943)

We must work passionately and indefatigably[1] to bridge the gulf[2] between our scientific progress and our moral progress. One of the great problems of mankind is that we suffer from a poverty of the spirit which stands in glaring[3] contrast to our scientific and technological abundance. The richer we have become materially, the poorer we have become morally and spiritually.

Every man lives in two realms, the internal and the external. The internal is that realm of spiritual ends expressed in art, literature, morals and religion. The external is that complex[4] of devices[5], techniques, mechanisms[6] and instrumentalities[7] by means of which we live.

Our problem today is that we have allowed the internal to become lost in the external. We have allowed the means by which we live to outdistance[8] the ends for which we live. So much of modern life can be summarized in that suggestive phrase of Thoreau: "Improved means to an unimproved end." This is the serious predicament[9], the deep and haunting[10] problem, confronting modern man.

Enlarged material powers spell[11] enlarged peril[12] if there is not proportionate[13] growth of the soul. When the external of man's nature subjugates[14] the internal, dark storm clouds begin to form.

Martin Luther King (1929-1968):
Where Do We Go From Here: Chaos or Community?

1. indefatigably [ˌɪndɪˈfætɪɡəbəli] (adv.) with sustained enthusiastic action and tireless energy 不厭倦地
2. gulf [ɡʌlf] (n.) an important difference between the ideas, opinions, or situations of two groups of people 巨大分歧；鴻溝
3. glaring [ˈɡlerɪŋ] (a.) easily perceived or detected 明顯的
4. complex [kɑːmˈpleks] (n.) a whole composed of various interrelated parts 複合物；綜合體
5. device [dɪˈvaɪs] (n.) a tool or machine designed to perform a particular task or function 設備；儀器
6. mechanism [ˈmekənɪzəm] (n.) a part of a machine, or a set of parts that work together 機械裝置
7. instrumentality [ˌɪnstruːmenˈtælɪti] (n.) a means; an agency 手段
8. outdistance [aʊtˈdɪstəns] (v.) to be faster in a race than other competitors, or to be much better than someone 大大超過
9. predicament [prɪˈdɪkəmənt] (n.) an unpleasant situation which is difficult to get out of 尷尬的處境；困境
10. haunting [ˈhɑːntɪŋ] (a.) continually recurring to the mind; unforgettable 縈繞於心頭的；不易忘懷的
11. spell [spel] (v.) to cause something bad to happen in the future 招致；帶來
12. peril [ˈperəl] (n.) imminent danger （嚴重的）危險
13. proportionate [prəˈpɔːrʃənɪt] (a.) adjusted according to a certain relation 成比例的；相稱的
14. subjugate [ˈsʌbdʒuɡɪt] (v.) to bring somebody, especially a people or nation, under the control of another 征服；制服

8| Social Problems

These are the issues that concern us today: the prevention of war; the protection of the environment; the balancing of population and resources; the management of energy so that we will neither exhaust our resources with unbridled[1] growth nor contaminate[2] the environment; the distribution[3] of resources among nations and groups who have been differently dowered[4] in the past by nature and history; the humanization of technology so that technology can be used for human ends and not primarily for profit or for power; the replanning of towns and cities so that neighborhoods can again be a microcosm[5] of three-generational wholeness of life; the creation of transcendental[6] values that will no longer set members of one religion against another, or of one ideology[7] against another, so that all human beings can move in new ways without being traitors to the old. Of these, only the need to prevent war was as clear to me then as it is now.

Perhaps most important of all, I did not have any doubt then that the world was changing, that change was in the very air we breathed, absolutely unpreventable and absolutely necessary. I think this too is part of the quality of life, that human beings must have a chance to learn to cherish the past, act in the present, and leave the future open.

↗ Margaret Mead (1901-1978):
Reflections on the Human Condition

1. unbridled [ʌnˈbraɪdld] (a.) freely and openly expressed 無拘束的
2. contaminate [kənˈtæmɪneɪt] (v.) to spoil the purity of something or make it poisonous 汙染；毒害
3. distribution [ˌdɪstrɪˈbjuːʃən] (n.) the handing out or delivery of things to a number of people 分配
4. dower [ˈdaʊər] (v.) to endow somebody with something 給予；賦予
5. microcosm [ˌmaɪkroʊkɑːzəm] (n.) a small place, society, or situation which has the same characteristics as something much larger 小宇宙；（作為宇宙縮影的）人類
6. transcendental [ˌtrænsenˈdentl] (a.) relating to mystical or supernatural experience and therefore beyond the material world 超越的
7. ideology [ˌaɪdiˈɑːlədʒi] (n.) a theory, or set of beliefs or principles, especially one on which a political system, party, or organization is based 思想體系；意識形態

82 The Twentieth Century

🎧 82 🎧 The marriage of reason and nightmare which has dominated the 20th century has given birth to an ever more ambiguous[1] world. Across the communications landscape move the specters[2] of sinister[3] technologies and the dreams that money can buy. Thermonuclear[4] weapons systems and soft drink commercials[5] coexist in an overlit[6] realm ruled by advertising and pseudo-events[7], science and pornography[8]. Over our lives preside[9] the great twin leitmotifs[10] of the 20th century—sex and paranoia[11].

↗ James Graham Ballard (1930-2009):
Introduction, 1974, to the French edition of Crash

1. ambiguous [æm'bɪgjuəs] (a.) causing uncertainty or confusion
   含糊不清的；引起歧義的
2. specter ['spɛktər] (n.) a ghostly presence or apparition 鬼怪；幽靈
3. sinister ['sɪnɪstər] (a.) wicked or dishonorable 邪惡的；不幸的
4. thermonuclear [,θɜːrmoʊ'nuːkliər] (a.) relating to or making use of nuclear fusion〔核〕熱核的
5. commercial [kə'mɜːrʃəl] (n.) an advertisement which is broadcast on television or radio（電視、廣播中的）商業廣告
6. overlit [,oʊvər'lɪt] (a.) too light or frivolous 過亮的
7. pseudo-event ['sjuːdəʊɪ'vɛnt] (n.) an event that has been caused to occur or staged to engender press coverage and public interest 〔口〕假事件（為製造新聞而導演出來的事件）
8. pornography [pɔːr'nɑːgrəfi] (n.) obscene writings or pictures 色情書刊、電影等色情描寫
9. preside [prɪ'zaɪd] (v.) to possess or exercise authority or control 管轄；指揮（preside over ...）
10. leitmotif ['laɪtmoʊ,tiːf] (n.) a recurring theme, e.g. in literature or history〔德〕主旨；主題
11. paranoia [,pærə'nɔɪə] (n.) an extreme and unreasonable feeling that other people do not like you or are going to harm or criticize you 〔醫〕偏執狂；妄想狂

Erich Fromm (1900-1980)

83 Modern Man

Modern man, if he dared to be articulate[1] about his concept of heaven, would describe a vision which would look like the biggest department store in the world, showing new things and gadgets[2], and himself having plenty of money with which to buy them. He would wander around open-mouthed in this heaven of gadgets and commodities[3], provided only that there were ever more and newer things to buy, and perhaps that his neighbors were just a little less privileged[4] than he.

↗ Erich Fromm (1900-1980):
The Sane Society

1. articulate [ɑːrˈtɪkjʊleɪt] (v.) to express in words 明確表達
2. gadget [ˈgædʒɪt] (n.) a small device that performs or aids a simple task 小巧的器具、裝置
3. commodity [kəˈmɑːdəti] (n.) a substance or product that can be traded, bought or sold 商品
4. privileged [ˈprɪvɪlɪdʒd] (a.) enjoying privileges, especially the resources and advantages associated with the upper classes or the rich 享有特權的

84 Cities and City Life

🎧 84 ⏵ Living in cities is an art, and we need the vocabulary of art, of style, to describe the peculiar relationship between man and material that exists in the continual creative play of urban living. The city as we imagine it, then, soft of illusion, myth, aspiration, and nightmare, is as real, maybe more real, than the hard city one can locate on maps in statistics, in monographs[1] on urban sociology[2] and demography[3] and architecture[4].

↗ Jonathan Raban (b. 1942):
Soft City

85 Poverty and the Poor

We have grown literally[5] afraid to be poor. We despise[6] anyone who elects to be poor in order to simplify and save his inner life. If he does not join the general scramble[7] and pant[8] with the money-making street, we deem[9] him spiritless[10] and lacking in ambition.

↗ William James (1842-1910):
The Varieties of Religious Experience

1. monograph ['mɑːnəgræf] (n.) a long article or a short book on a particular subject 專題論文
2. sociology [ˌsoʊsi'ɑːlədʒi] (n.) the study of the relationships between people living in groups, especially in industrial societies 社會學
3. demography [dɪ'mɑːgrəfi] (n.) the study of human populations, including their size, growth, density, and distribution, and statistics regarding birth, marriage, disease, and death 人口統計學
4. architecture ['ɑːrkɪtektʃər] (n.) the art and science of designing and constructing buildings 建築學
5. literally ['lɪtərəli] (adv.) used to show that a statement is actually true and not exaggerated 實在地；不誇張地
6. despise [dɪ'spaɪz] (v.) to feel a strong dislike for someone or something because you think they are bad or worthless 鄙視
7. scramble ['skræmbəl] (n.) a jumbled mass of people or things 混亂的一團
8. pant [pænt] (v.) to breathe rapidly in short gasps 喘氣
9. deem [diːm] (v.) to judge or consider something in a particular light 視作；認為
10. spiritless ['spɪrɪtləs] (a.) lacking energy and enthusiasm 無生氣的

86 Universe

86 The universe, so far as we can observe it, is a wonderful and immense[1] engine; its extent, its order, its beauty, its cruelty, make it alike impressive. If we dramatize[2] its life and conceive[3] its spirit, we are filled with wonder, terror, and amusement, so magnificent is that spirit, so prolific[4], inexorable[5], grammatical[6], and dull. Like all animals and plants, the cosmos has its own way of doing things, not wholly rational[7] nor ideally best, but patient, fatal, and fruitful. Great is this organism[8] of mud and fire, terrible this vast, painful, glorious experiment.

The Creation of Adam (Michelangelo, 1475-1564)

Why should we not look on the universe with piety? Is it not our substance? Are we made of other clay[9]? All our possibilities lie from eternity[10] hidden in its bosom. It is the dispenser[11] of all our joys.

We may address it without superstitious[12] terrors; it is not wicked[13]. It follows its own habits abstractedly; it can be trusted to be true to its word.

Society is not impossible between it and us, and since it is the source of all our energies, the home of all our happiness, shall we not cling to it and praise it, seeing that it vegetates[14] so grandly[15] and so sadly, and that it is not for us to blame it for what, doubtless, it never knew that it did?

↗ George Santayana (1863-1952):
Reason in Religion

1. immense [ɪˈmɛns] (a.) extremely large in size or degree 巨大的；廣大的
2. dramatize [ˈdræmətaɪz] (v.) to make something more dramatic, especially to exaggerate the importance or seriousness of a situation in an attention-seeking and theatrical way 使戲劇化
3. conceive [kənˈsiːv] (v.) to form or develop in the mind; devise 構想出；想像；設想
4. prolific [prəˈlɪfɪk] (a.) producing ideas or works frequently and in large quantities 多產的；富於創造力的
5. inexorable [ɪnˈɛksərəbəl] (a.) not moved by anyone's attempts to plead or persuade 無法改變的；不可阻擋的
6. grammatical [grəˈmætɪkəl] (a.) conforming to the rules of grammar 合乎文法的；文法正確的
7. rational [ˈræʃənəl] (a.) having or exercising the ability to reason 理性的；合理的
8. organism [ˈɔːrgənɪzəm] (n.) a single living plant, animal, virus, etc. 有機體
9. clay [kleɪ] (n.) the physical body of a human being, particularly the matter of which it is composed（上帝造人的）泥土
10. eternity [ɪˈtɜːrnəti] (n.) time which never ends or which has no limits 永恆；不朽
11. dispenser [dɪˈspɛnsər] (n.) somebody or something that distributes something 分配者；施與者
12. superstitious [ˌsuːpərˈstɪʃəs] (a.) convinced that performing or not performing specific actions brings good or bad luck, that some events or phenomena are omens, and, generally, fearfully believing in a supernatural dimension to events 因迷信而形成的
13. wicked [ˈwɪkɪd] (a.) evil by nature and in practice 壞的；邪惡的
14. vegetate [ˈvɛdʒɪteɪt] (v.) to live or behave in a dull, inactive, or undemanding way 像植物般生長；茫然地過活
15. grandly [ˈgrændli] (adv.) in an outstanding and impressive way 宏偉地；盛大地

Spring, High Water (Isaak Levitan, 1860-1900)

87 Nature's Ultrahumanity

Achieving a relationship with nature is both a science and an art, beyond mere knowledge or mere feeling alone; and, I now think, beyond Oriental[1] mysticism[2], transcendentalism[3], "Meditation[4] techniques," and the rest—or at least as we in the West have converted[5] them to our use, which seems increasingly in a narcissistic[6] way: to make ourselves feel more positive, more meaningful, more dynamic[7].

The Knight of the Flowers (Georges Antoine Rochegrosse, 1859-1938)

I do not believe nature is to be reached that way either, by turning it into a therapy[8], a free clinic[9] for admirers of their own sensitivity.

The subtlest of our alienations[10] from it, the most difficult to comprehend[11], is our eternal need to use it in some way, to derive[12] some personal yield. We shall never fully understand nature (or ourselves), and certainly never respect it, until we dissociate[13] the wild from the notion[14] of usability—however innocent and harmless the use. For it is the general uselessness of so much of nature that lies at the foot of our ancient hostility[15] and indifference to it.

↗ John Fowles (1926-2005):
The Tree

1. Oriental [ˌɔːriˈentəl] (a.) relating to the countries and peoples of East Asia, especially China, Japan, and neighboring countries （大寫）東方的；亞洲的

2. mysticism [ˈmɪstɪsɪzəm] (n.) the belief that there is hidden meaning in life or that each human being can unite with God 神秘主義；玄想

3. transcendentalism [ˌtrænsenˈdentəlɪzəm] (n.) a literary and philosophical movement, associated with Ralph Waldo Emerson and Margaret Fuller, asserting the existence of an ideal spiritual reality that transcends the empirical and scientific and is knowable through intuition 〔哲〕超越論；先驗論

4. meditation [ˌmedɪˈteɪʃən] (n.) the emptying of the mind of thoughts, or the concentration of the mind on one thing, in order to aid mental or spiritual development, contemplation, or relaxation 〔宗〕冥想

5. convert [kənˈvɜːrt] (v.) to (cause something or someone to) change in form, character, or opinion 轉變；變換

6. narcissistic [ˌnɑːrsɪˈsɪstɪk] (a.) excessive love or admiration of oneself 自我陶醉的

7. dynamic [daɪˈnæmɪk] (a.) full of energy, enthusiasm, and a sense of purpose and able both to get things going and to get things done 有活力的；強有力的

8. therapy [ˈθerəpi] (n.) treatment of physical, mental, or behavioral problems that is meant to cure or rehabilitate somebody 療法

9. clinic [ˈklɪnɪk] (n.) a building, often part of a hospital, to which people can go for medical care or advice 診所；門診所

10. alienation [ˌeɪliəˈneɪʃən] (n.) the feeling that you have no connection with the people around you 疏離

11. comprehend [ˌkɑːmprɪˈhend] (v.) to grasp the meaning or nature of something 理解；瞭解

12. derive [dɪˈraɪv] (v.) to get or obtain something from something else 衍生出；得到

13. dissociate [dɪˈsouʃieɪt] (v.) to consider as separate and not related 使分離；將⋯⋯分開

14. notion [ˈnouʃən] (n.) a belief or opinion 觀念；想法

15. hostility [hɑːˈstɪləti] (n.) a feeling or attitude of hatred, enmity, antagonism, or anger toward somebody 敵意；敵視

88 The Sympathy of Nature

Such was the sympathy of Nature—that wild, heathen[1] Nature of the forest, never subjugated[2] by human law, nor illumined[3] by higher truth . . . Love, whether newly born, or aroused from a death-like slumber[4], must always create a sunshine, filling the heart so full of radiance[5], that it overflows upon the outward world.

↗ Nathaniel Hawthorne (1804-1864):
The Scarlet Letter

1. heathen ['hiːðən] (a.) not acknowledging the God of Christianity and Judaism and Islam 未開化的
2. subjugate ['sʌbdʒυgɪt] (v.) to bring somebody, especially a people or nation, under the control of another 屈從；征服
3. illumine [ɪ'luːmɪn] (v.) same as illuminate, to enlighten intellectually or spiritually 啟發；啟迪
4. slumber ['slʌmbər] (n.) to be asleep 睡眠
5. radiance ['reɪdɪəns] (n.) joy, energy, or good health discernible in somebody's face or demeanor 光輝；欣喜

Henri Martin (1860-1943)

89 Real Enjoyment

🎧 89 🎧　All real and wholesome[1] enjoyments possible to man have been just as possible to him, since first he was made of the earth, as they are now; and they are possible to him chiefly in peace. To watch the corn grow, and the blossoms set[2]; to draw hard breath over ploughshade[3] or spade[4]; to read, to think, to love, to hope, to pray—these are the things that make men happy . . . Now and then a wearied king, or a tormented slave, found out where the true kingdoms of the world were, and possessed himself, in a furrow[5] or two of garden ground, of a truly infinite dominion[6].

↗ John Ruskin (1819-1900):
Modern Painters

1. wholesome ['hoʊlsəm] (a.) beneficial to physical health, usually by virtue of being fresh and naturally produced 有益於身心健康的；有益的
2. set [set] (v.) to produce, as after pollination（植物）結果
3. ploughshade ['plaʊʃeɪd] (n.) a broad curved blade of a plough 鏵
4. spade [speɪd] (n.) a digging tool with a wide shallow blade flattened where it meets the shaft so it can be pushed into the ground with the foot 鏟；鍬
5. furrow ['fʌroʊ] (n.) a long line or hollow which is formed or cut into the surface of something 犁溝
6. dominion [də'mɪnjən] (n.) the land that belongs to a ruler 領地；領土

Henri Martin (1860-1943)

90 Experience

🎧 90　Experience is not a matter of having actually swum the Hellespont[1], or danced with the dervishes[2], or slept in a doss-house[3]. It is a matter of sensibility and intuition, of seeing and hearing the significant things, of paying attention at the right moments, of understanding and coordinating[4]. Experience is not what happens to a man; it is what a man does with what happens to him.

↗ Aldous Huxley (1894-1963):

Texts and Pretexts

1. Hellespont: the ancient name of a narrow strait in northwestern Turkey connecting the Aegean Sea to the Sea of Marmara, now known by the modern European term "the Dardanelles." 即今天的達達尼爾海峽
2. dervish ['dɜːrvɪʃ] (n.) a member of a Muslim religious group which has an energetic dance as part of its worship 托缽僧；苦行僧
3. doss-house: a cheap hotel or rooming house 供流浪漢投宿的廉價客棧
4. coordinate [koʊ'ɔːrdɪneɪt] (v.) to organize a complex enterprise in which numerous people are involved and bring their contributions together to form a coherent or efficient whole 協力；協調

Virginia Woolf (1882-1941)

91 | Thought and Thinking

We all indulge[1] in the strange, pleasant process called thinking, but when it comes to saying, even to someone opposite, what we think, then how little we are able to convey[2]! The phantom[3] is through the mind and out of the window before we can lay salt on its tail, or slowly sinking and returning to the profound darkness which it has lit up momentarily[4] with a wandering[5] light.

↗ Virginia Woolf (1882-1941):
The Common Reader

1. indulge [ɪn'dʌldʒ] (v.) to allow yourself or somebody else to experience something enjoyable 沉迷於
2. convey [kən'veɪ] (v.) to express a thought, feeling or idea so that it is understood by other people 傳達；表達
3. phantom ['fæntəm] (n.) a ghost or apparition 幽靈；鬼魂
4. momentarily [ˌmoʊmən'terɪli] (adv.) for a moment or an instant 短暫地
5. wandering ['wɑːndərɪŋ] (a.) migratory 蜿蜒的；曲折的

Portrait of the Artist Surrounded by Masks
(James Ensor, 1860-1949)

92 Difference of Opinion

One lesson we learn early, that in spite of seeming difference, men are all of one pattern. We readily assume this with our mates, and are disappointed and angry if we find that we are premature[1], and that their watches are slower than ours. In fact, the only sin which we never forgive in each other is difference of opinion.

↗ Ralph Waldo Emerson (1803-1882):
Society and Solitude

93 Conservatives and Radicals

Men are conservatives[2] when they are least vigorous[3], or when they are most luxurious[4]. They are conservatives after dinner, or before taking their rest; when they are sick or aged. In the morning, or when their intellect or their conscience has been aroused, when they hear music, or when they read poetry, they are radicals[5].

↗ Ralph Waldo Emerson (1803-1882):
New England Reformers

1. premature [ˌpriːməˈtʃʊr] (a.) occurring, existing, or developing earlier than is expected, normal, or advisable 不成熟的；過早的
2. conservative [kənˈsɜːrvətɪv] (n.) one favoring traditional views and values 保守者
3. vigorous [ˈvɪgərəs] (a.) displaying or using great energy 強而有力的
4. luxurious [lʌgˈʒʊəriəs] (a.) with a liking for luxury, or used to living in luxury 奢侈的
5. radical [ˈrædɪkəl] (n.) somebody with radical views on political, economic, or social issues 激進分子

94 Conscience

When I contemplate[1] the accumulation of guilt and remorse[2] which, like a garbage-can, I carry through life, and which is fed not only by the lightest action but by the most harmless pleasure, I feel Man to be of all living things the most biologically incompetent[3] and ill-organized.

Why has he acquired a seventy years' lifespan only to poison it incurably[4] by the mere being of himself?

Why has he thrown Conscience, like a dead rat, to putrefy[5] in the well?

↗ Cyril Connolly (1903-1974):
The Unquiet Grave

1. contemplate [ˈkɑːntəmpleɪt] (v.) to spend time considering a possible future action, or to consider one particular thing for a long time in a serious and quiet way 仔細考慮；思量
2. remorse [rɪˈmɔːrs] (n.) a strong feeling of guilt and regret 自責；痛悔
3. incompetent [ɪnˈkɑːmpɪtənt] (a.) lacking the skills, qualities, or ability to do something properly 無能力的；不適任的
4. incurably [ɪnˈkjʊrəbəli] (adv.) in a manner impossible to cure 無法治癒地
5. putrefy [ˈpjuːtrɪfaɪ] (v.) to decay, producing a strong unpleasant smell 使腐敗；使墮落

95 Silence

Silence is the universal refuge, the sequel[1] to all dull discourses and all foolish acts, a balm[2] to our every chagrin[3], as welcome after satiety[4] as after disappointment; that background which the painter may not daub[5], be he master or bungler[6], and which, however awkward a figure we may have made in the foreground, remains ever our inviolable[7] asylum[8], where no indignity[9] can assail[10], no personality can disturb us.

↗ Henry D. Thoreau (1817-1862):
A Week on the Concord and Merrimac Rivers

1. sequel ['siːkwəl] (n.) an event which happens after and is the result of an earlier event 隨之而來的事；結局
2. balm [bɑːlm] (n.) something that gives comfort 安慰（物）；慰藉（物）
3. chagrin [ʃə'grɪn] (n.) a feeling of vexation or humiliation due to disappointment about something 懊惱；悔恨
4. satiety [sə'taɪəti] (n.) the condition of being full or gratified beyond the point of satisfaction 飽足；滿足
5. daub [dɑːb] (v.) to spread a thick or sticky liquid on something or to cover something with a thick or sticky liquid, often quickly or carelessly 塗抹；塗鴉
6. bungler ['bʌŋglər] (n.) someone who makes mistakes because of incompetence 笨拙者；經驗不夠的人
7. inviolable [ɪn'vaɪələbəl] (a.) which must not or cannot be broken, damaged or doubted 不可侵犯的
8. asylum [ə'saɪləm] (n.) protection from danger or imminent harm provided by a sheltered place 避難所；庇護所
9. indignity [ɪn'dɪgnɪti] (n.) a situation that results in a humiliating loss of dignity or self-esteem 侮辱言行；無禮舉動
10. assail [ə'seɪl] (v.) to attack someone violently or criticize someone strongly 襲擊；困擾

96 Satire

Satire[1] is a sort of glass wherein beholders do generally discover everybody's face but their own; which is the chief reason for that kind reception it meets with in the world, and that so very few are offended with it. But, if it should happen otherwise, the danger is not great; and I have learned from long experience never to apprehend[2] mischief from those whose understanding I have been able to provoke[3]: for anger and fury, though they add strength to the sinews[4] of the body, yet are found to relax those of the mind, and to render all its efforts feeble and impotent[5].

↗ Jonathan Swift (1667-1745):
The Battle of the Books

1. satire ['sætaɪr] (n.) a way of criticizing people or ideas in a humorous way, or a piece of writing or play which uses this style 諷刺文學
2. apprehend [ˌæprɪ'hend] (v.) to understand something 理解；領會
3. provoke [prə'voʊk] (v.) to be the cause or occasion of an emotion or response 激起；導致
4. sinew ['sɪnjuː] (n.) a tendon, a strong cord in the body connecting a muscle to a bone 腱
5. impotent ['ɪmpətənt] (a.) without the strength or power to do anything effective or helpful 虛弱的；無力的

Afternoon Rest (James Smetham, 1821-1889)

97 Idleness

Idleness predominates[1] in many lives where it is not suspected; for, being a vice[2] which terminates in itself, it may be enjoyed without injury to others; and it is therefore not watched like fraud[3], which endangers property; or like pride, which naturally seeks its gratifications in another's inferiority[4]. Idleness is a silent and peaceful quality, that neither raises envy by ostentation[5], nor hatred by opposition; and therefore nobody is busy to censure[6] or detect[7] it.

↗ Samuel Johnson (1709-1784):
Idleness

98 Hate

There is no hate without fear. Hate is crystallized[8] fear, fear's dividend[9], fear objectivized. We hate what we fear and so where hate is, fear is lurking[10]. Thus we hate what threatens our person, our liberty, our privacy, our income, our popularity, our vanity[11] and our dreams and plans for ourselves. If we can isolate[12] this element in what we hate we may be able to cease from hating.

↗ Cyril Connolly (1903-1974):
The Unquiet Grave

1. predominate [prɪˈdɑːmɪneɪt] (v.) to dominate or control somebody or something 主宰；支配
2. vice [vaɪs] (n.) an immoral or wicked habit or characteristic 罪行
3. fraud [frɔːd] (n.) something that is intended to deceive people 騙局
4. inferiority [ɪnˌfɪriˈɔːrɪti] (n.) the state of being inferior, of or characteristic of low rank or importance 自卑感
5. ostentation [ˌɑːstənˈteɪʃən] (n.) conspicuous or vulgar display of wealth and success, especially designed to impress people 賣弄；虛飾
6. censure [ˈsenʃər] (v.) to make a formal, often public statement of disapproval of somebody or something 責備
7. detect [dɪˈtekt] (v.) to discover (something obscure); to bring to light 察覺
8. crystallize [ˈkrɪstəlaɪz] (v.) to give a definite, precise, and usually permanent form to 結晶；成形
9. dividend [ˈdɪvɪdənd] (n.) something good or desirable that is gained as a bonus along with something else 贈品
10. lurk [lɜːrk] (v.) to exist although it is not always noticeable 潛伏
11. vanity [ˈvænəti] (n.) excessive pride, especially in personal appearance 虛榮
12. isolate [ˈaɪsəleɪt] (v.) to separate somebody or something from others of the same type 隔離；脫離

99 The Beloved

Now, the beloved can also be of any description. The most outlandish[1] people can be the stimulus[2] for love. A man may be a doddering[3] great grandfather and still love only a strange girl he saw in the streets of Cheehaw one afternoon two decades past. The preacher may love a fallen woman. The beloved may be treacherous[4], greasy-headed, and given to evil habits. Yes, and the lover may see this as clearly as anyone else—but that does not affect the evolution of his love one whit[5].

A most mediocre[6] person can be the object of a love which is wild, extravagant, and beautiful as the poison lilies of the swamp[7]. A good man may be the stimulus for a love both violent and debased[8], or a jabbering[9] madman may bring about in the soul of someone a tender and simple idyll[10]. Therefore, the value and quality of any love is determined solely by the lover himself.

1. outlandish [aʊt'lændɪʃ] (a.) alien or foreign 異國風格的
2. stimulus ['stɪmjʊləs] (n.) an agent, action, or condition that elicits or accelerates a physiological/psychological activity or response 刺激物
3. doddering ['dɔːdərɪŋ] (a.) infirm, feeble, and often senile（因年老而）變衰弱的
4. treacherous ['tretʃərəs] (a.) betraying a trust 背叛的
5. whit [wɪt] (n.) the smallest particle（多用於否定句中）一點點；絲毫
6. mediocre [ˌmiːdi'oʊkər] (a.) moderate to inferior in quality 平凡的
7. swamp [swɑːmp] (n.) very wet soft land 沼澤；沼澤地
8. debased [dɪ'beɪst] (a.) ruined in character or quality 貶抑的；不名譽的
9. jabbering ['dʒæbərɪŋ] (a.) rapid and indistinct speech 話說得快而含糊的
10. idyll ['aɪdl] (n.) a short work in verse or prose, a painting, or a piece of music depicting simple pastoral or rural scenes and the life of country folk, often in an idealized way 田園詩；田園散文

The Wedding of Saint George and the Princess Sabra
(Dante Gabriel Rossetti, 1828-1882)

It is for this reason that most of us would rather love than be loved. Almost everyone wants to be the lover. And the curt[11] truth is that, in a deep secret way, the state of being beloved is intolerable to many. The beloved fears and hates the lover, and with the best of reasons. For the lover is forever trying to strip bare his beloved. The lover craves[12] any possible relation with the beloved, even if this experience can cause him only pain.

↗ Carson McCullers (1917-1967):
The Ballad of the Sad Cafe

---

11. curt [kɜːrt] (a.) using few words 簡明扼要的
12. crave [kreɪv] (v.) to have an intense desire for 渴望

Eros (Sidney Harold Meteyard, 1868-1947)

100 Love

Madame, it is an old word and each one takes it new and wears it out himself. It is a word that fills with meaning as a bladder[1] with air and the meaning goes out of it as quickly. It may be punctured as a bladder is punctured and patched[2] and blown up again and if you have not had it it does not exist for you. All people talk of it, but those who have had it are marked by it, and I would not wish to speak of it further since of all things it is the most ridiculous to talk of and only fools go through it many times.

↗ Ernest Hemingway (1899-1961): *Death in the Afternoon*

1. bladder [ˈblædər] (n.) an inflatable part of something, especially a football, that resembles a bag 囊袋
2. patch [pætʃ] (v.) to put a patch, a small piece of material fixed over something for covering, on something 修補

Wrestling (Emile Friant, 1863-1932)

101 Youth and Lost

Youth in the outset[1] of life (and particularly at this time I felt it so) our imagination has a body to it. We are in a state between sleeping and waking, and have indistinct[2] but glorious glimpses[3] of strange shapes, and there is always something to come better than what we see.

As in our dreams the fullness of the blood gives warmth and reality to the coinage[4] of the brain, so in youth our ideas are clothed, and fed, and pampered[5] with our good spirits; we breathe thick with thoughtless happiness, the weight of future years presses on the strong pulses of the heart, and we repose[6] with undisturbed faith in truth and good.

As we advance, we exhaust out fund of enjoyment and of hope. We are no longer wrapped in lamb's-wool, lulled[7] in Elysium[8]. As we taste the pleasures of life, their spirit evaporates[9], the sense palls[10]; and nothing is left but the phantoms[11], the lifeless shadows of what has been!

↗ William Hazlitt (1778-1830):
My First Acquaintance With Poets

1. outset ['aʊtset] (n.) the beginning or initial stage of an activity 最初
2. indistinct [ˌɪndɪ'stɪŋkt] (a.) not seen or heard clearly 不清楚的；模糊的
3. glimpse [glɪmps] (n.) when you see something or someone for a very short time 瞥見；一瞥
4. coinage ['kɔɪnɪdʒ] (n.) the invention of a new word or phrase in a language（新詞的）創造
5. pamper ['pæmpər] (v.) treat with excessive indulgence 縱容；嬌養
6. repose [rɪ'poʊz] (v.) to be supported or based on something 把（希望等）寄託於
7. lull [lʌl] (v.) to soothe or calm a person or animal, especially by using gentle sounds or motions 使平靜
8. Elysium [ɪ'lɪzɪəm] (n.) in Greek mythology, the home of the blessed after death〔希神〕樂園；天堂
9. evaporate [ɪ'væpəreɪt] (v.) to disappear 消失；消散
10. pall [pɑːl] (v.) to be or become uninteresting, unsatisfying, or insipid 感到乏味；厭倦
11. phantom ['fæntəm] (n.) something existing in perception only 有名無實的人或物

Summer Scene (Jean Frederic Bazille, 1841-1870)

102 Age

🎧102 The same space seems shorter as we grow older . . .
in youth we may have an absolutely new experience,
subjective or objective, every hour of the day.
Apprehension[1] is vivid, retentiveness[2] strong, and our
recollections[3] of that time, like those of a time spent in
rapid and interesting travel, are of something intricate[4],
multitudinous[5], and long-drawn out. But as each passing
year converts[6] some of this experience into automatic
routine which we hardly note at all, the days and the week
smooth themselves out in recollection to contentless units,
and years grow hollow and collapse[7].

William James (1842-1910):
Principles of Psychology

1. apprehension [ˌæprɪ'henʃən] (n.) anxiety about the future or a fear that
   something unpleasant is going to happen 恐懼;憂慮
2. retentiveness [rɪ'tentɪvnəs] (n.) the power of retaining and recalling past
   experience 記性好
3. recollection [ˌrekə'lekʃən] (n.) a memory of something 回憶;記憶
4. intricate ['ɪntrɪkɪt] (a.) containing many details or small parts that are
   combined in a particularly complex or skillful way 錯綜複雜的
5. multitudinous [ˌmʌltɪ'tuːdɪnəs] (a.) including many parts, items, or
   features 種類繁多的
6. convert [kən'vɜːrt] (v.) to (cause something or someone to) change in
   form, character, or opinion 變換;轉變
7. collapse [kə'læps] (v.) to fail or come to an end suddenly 崩潰;瓦解

Death (Jacek Malczewski, 1854-1929)

103 How to Grow Old

Psychologically there are two dangers to be guarded against in old age. One of these is undue[1] absorption[2] in the past. It does not do to live in memories, in regrets for the good old days, or in sadness about friends who are dead. One's thought must be directed to the future, and to things about which there is something to be done.

This is not always easy; one's own past is a gradually increasing weight. It is easy to think to oneself that one's emotions used to be more vivid than they are, and one's mind more keen[3]. If this is true it should be forgotten, and if it is forgotten it will probably not be true.

The other thing to be avoided is clinging[4] to youth in the hope of sucking vigor from it's vitality[5]. When your children are grown up they want to live their own lives, and if you continued to be as interested in them as you were when they were young, you are likely to become a burden of them, unless they are unusually callous[6]. I do not mean that one should be without interest in them, but one's interest should be contemplative[7] and, if possible, philanthropic[8], but not unduly emotional.

↗ Bertrand Russell (1872-1970)

1. undue [ʌn'duː] (a.) going beyond the limits of what is proper, normal, justified, or permitted 過度的;過分的
2. absorption [əb'sɔːrpʃən] (n.) a state in which the whole attention is occupied 全神貫注;專心致志(absorption in . . .)
3. keen [kiːn] (a.) acutely sensitive 敏銳的
4. cling [klɪŋ] (v.) to stick onto or hold something or someone tightly, or to refuse to stop holding them 依靠;依附
5. vitality [vaɪ'tæləti] (n.) abundant physical and mental energy 活力;生氣
6. callous ['kæləs] (a.) emotionally hardened; unfeeling 無感覺的;麻木不仁的
7. contemplative ['kɑːntem,pleɪtɪv] (a.) calm and thoughtful, or inclined to be this way 沉思的;冥想的
8. philanthropic [,fɪlən'θrɑːpɪk] (a.) helping poor people, especially by giving them money 博愛的;仁慈的

4 Stories & Fables

Rachel Carson (1907-1964)

104 A Spring Without Voices

🎧104 Then a strange blight[1] crept over the area and everything began to change. Some evil spell had settled on the community: mysterious maladies[2] swept the flocks of chickens; the cattle and sheep sickened and died. Everywhere was a shadow of death. The farmers spoke of much illness among their families. In the town the doctors had become more and more puzzled by new kinds of sickness appearing among their patients.

There had been several sudden and unexplained deaths, not only adults but even among children, who would be stricken suddenly while at play and die within a few hours.

There was strange stillness. The birds, for example— where had they gone? Many people spoke of them, puzzled and disturbed. The feeding stations in the backyards were deserted. The few birds seen anywhere were moribund[3]. They trembled violently and could not fly. It was a spring without voices. On the mornings that had once throbbed[4] with the dawn chorus[5] of robins, catbirds[6], doves, jays[7], wrens[8], and scores[9] of other bird voices there was now no sound. Only silence lay over the fields, woods and marsh[10].

↗ Rachel Carson (1907-1964):
Silent Spring

1. blight [blaɪt] (n.) a disease that damages and kills plants（植物）枯萎病
2. malady ['mælədi] (n.) a disease, a disorder, or an ailment 疾病
3. moribund ['mɔːrɪbʌnd] (a.) approaching death; about to die 垂死的
4. throb [θrɑːb] (v.) to produce a strong, regular beat 有節奏地震動
5. chorus ['kɔːrəs] (n.) a large group of singers who perform choral music or opera together 合唱
6. catbird ['kætbɜːrd] (n.) a North American songbird (Dumetella carolinensis) having predominantly slate plumage〔鳥〕貓鵲
7. jay [dʒeɪ] (n.) a bird of Europe and Asia with a pinkish-brown body and blue-and-black wings〔鳥〕松鴉
8. wren [ren] (n.) and of several small active brown birds of the northern hemisphere with short upright tails〔鳥〕鷦鷯
9. score [skɔːr] (n.) a great many 許多；大量
10. marsh [mɑːrʃ] (n.) ground near a lake, river or the sea, that tends to flood and is always wet 沼澤；濕地

The Wounded Hound (William Tylee Ranney, 1813-1857)

105 The Dog

  This man had saved his life, which was something; but, further, he was the ideal master. Other men saw to the welfare of their dogs from a sense of duty and business expediency[1]; he saw to the welfare of his as if they were his own children, because he could not help it. And he saw further. He never forgot a kindly greeting or a cheering word, and to sit down for a long talk with them—"gas[2]" he called it—was as much his delight as theirs.

↗ Jack London (1876-1916):
The Call of the Wild

---

1. expediency [ɪk'spiːdiənsi] (n.) when something is helpful or useful in a particular situation, but sometimes not morally acceptable 利己
2. gas [gæs] (n.) meaningless empty talk 空談

Good Friends (William Merritt Chase, 1849-1916)

106 Childhood

Childhood is less clear to me than to many people: when it ended I turned my face away from it for no reason that I know about, certainly without the usual reason of unhappy memories.

For many years that worried me, but then I discovered that the tales of former children are seldom to be trusted. Some people supply too many past victories or pleasures with which to comfort themselves, and other people cling to pains, real and imagined, to excuse what they have become.

I think I have always known about my memory. I know when it is to be trusted and when some dream or fantasy entered on the life, and the dream, the need of dream, led to distortion[1] of what happened. And so I knew early that the rampage[2] angers of an only child[3] were distorted nightmares of reality. But I trust absolutely what I remember about Julia.

↗ Lillian Hellman (1905-1984): *Julia*

---

1. distortion [dɪ'stɔːrʃən] (n.) the describing or reporting of something in a way that is inaccurate or misleading 扭曲
2. rampage [ræm'peɪdʒ] (n.) violent and usually wild behavior 暴跳；橫衝直撞
3. only child: a child who has no sisters or brothers 獨生子

Portrait of a Man Writing in His Study
(Gustave Caillebotte, 1848-1894)

107 Writers

He is a man of thirty-five, but looks fifty. He is bald, has varicose veins[1] and wears spectacles[2], or would wear them if his only pair were not chronically[3] lost. If things are normal with him, he will be suffering from malnutrition[4], but if he has recently had a lucky streak[5], he will be suffering from a hangover[6].

At present it is half past eleven in the morning, and according to his schedule he should have started work two hours ago; but even if he had made any serious effort to start he would have been frustrated by the almost continuous ringing of the telephone bell, the yells of the baby, the rattle[7] of an electric drill[8] out in the street, and the heavy boots of his creditors[9] clumping[10] up the stairs. The most recent interruption was the arrival of the second post, which brought him two circulars[11] and an income tax demand printed in red.

Needless to say this person is a writer.

↗ George Orwell (1903-1950):
Confessions of a Book Reviewer

1. varicose veins ['værɪkoʊs veɪnz] a swollen and often painful vein, especially in the legs〔醫〕靜脈曲張
2. spectacles ['spɛktəkəlz] (n.) a pair of glass or plastic lenses worn in a frame in front of the eyes to help correct imperfect vision〔舊〕眼鏡
3. chronically ['krɑːnɪkli] (adv.) in a habitual and long-standing manner 長期地
4. malnutrition [ˌmælnuˈtrɪʃən] (n.) a state of poor nutrition 營養失調
5. streak [striːk] (n.) a short period of good or bad luck（短暫的）一陣子；一點點
6. hangover ['hæŋoʊvər] (n.) a feeling of illness after drinking too much alcohol〔口〕宿醉
7. rattle ['rætl] (n.) a quick succession of short sharp knocking sounds, usually caused by something being moved or shaken 吵鬧聲
8. drill [drɪl] (n.) a tool or machine which makes holes 鑽；鑽頭
9. creditor ['krɛdɪtər] (n.) someone to whom money is owed 債權人
10. clump [klʌmp] (v.) to walk or move with a heavy thumping sound 以沉重的步伐行走
11. circular ['sɜːrkjʊlər] (n.) a single page leaflet advertising an event, a service, or other activity 傳單；公告

108 Happy Life

I grieve[1] to leave Thornfield: I love Thornfield:—I love it, because I have lived in it a full and delightful life,—momentarily[2] at least.

I have not been trampled[3] on. I have not been petrified[4]. I have not been buried with inferior[5] minds, and excluded[6] from every glimpse of communion[7] with what is bright and energetic and high. I have talked, face to face, with what I reverence[8], with what I delight in,—with an original, a vigorous, an expanded mind. I have known you, Mr. Rochester; and it strikes me with terror and anguish[9] to feel I absolutely must be torn from you forever, I see the necessity of departure[10]; and it is like looking on the necessity of death.

↗ Charlotte Bronte (1816-1855): Jane Eyre

1. grieve [griːv] (v.) to experience great sadness over something such as a death 悲傷；哀悼
2. momentarily [ˌmoʊmənˈterɪli] (adv.) a very short period of time 短暫地
3. trample [ˈtræmpəl] (v.) to tread heavily, or tread heavily on something or somebody so as to cause damage or injury 蔑視；傷害
4. petrify [ˈpetrɪfaɪ] (v.) to stun or paralyze with terror 使驚呆；把……嚇呆
5. inferior [ɪnˈfɪriər] (a.) lower, or of lower rank （地位等）低下的
6. exclude [ɪkˈskluːd] (v.) to prevent somebody or something from entering or participating 逐出；排除在外
7. communion [kəˈmjuːnjən] (n.) a relationship, especially one in which something is communicated or shared 融洽關係；密切配合
8. reverence [ˈrevərəns] (v.) a feeling of profound awe and respect and often love 敬愛；崇敬
9. anguish [ˈæŋgwɪʃ] (n.) extreme unhappiness caused by physical or mental suffering 極度的痛苦；苦惱
10. departure [dɪˈpɑːrtʃər] (n.) the action of setting off on a journey 離開

Elizabeth Winthrop Chanler (John Singer Sargent, 1856-192)

109 Day

🎧 109

The only exercise that Tess took at this time was after dark; and it was then, when out in the woods, that she seemed least solitary[1]. She knew how to hit to a hair's breadth[2] that moment of evening when the light and the darkness are so evenly balanced that the constraint[3] of day and the suspense[4] of night neutralize[5] each other, leaving absolute mental liberty. It is then that the plight[6] of being alive becomes attenuated[7] to its least possible dimensions.

She had no fear of the shadows; her sole idea seemed to be to shun[8] mankind—or rather that cold accretion[9] called the world, which, so terrible in the mass, is so unformidable[10], even pitiable, in its units.

↗ Thomas Hardy (1840-1928):
Tess of the D'Urbervilles

1. solitary ['sɑːləteri] (a.) done without the company of other people 獨自的；孤獨的
2. hair's breadth: a very small margin or distance 間不容髮；很短的距離
3. constraint [kən'streɪnt] (n.) something that limits freedom of action 約束；抑制
4. suspense [sə'spens] (n.) the feeling of excitement or anxiety which you have when you are waiting for something to happen and are uncertain about what it is going to be 掛慮；懸念
5. neutralize ['nuːtrəlaɪz] (v.) to counterbalance or counteract the effect of 抵銷；中和
6. plight [plaɪt] (n.) a difficult or dangerous situation, especially a sad or desperate predicament 困境
7. attenuated [ə'tenjueɪt] (a.) weakened 減弱的；細長的
8. shun [ʃʌn] (v.) to avoid something 避開；迴避
9. accretion [ə'kriːʃən] (n.) an increase in size as a result of accumulation or the growing together of separate things 增加（物）
10. unformidable [ʌn'fɔːrmɪdəbəl] (a.) fearless; undreaded 不足以為懼的

A Hare in the Forest
(Hans Hoffmann, 1545-1592)

110 The Rabbits and the Wolves

Within the memory of the youngest child there was a family of rabbits who lived near a pack of wolves. The wolves announced that they did not like the way the rabbits were living. (The wolves were crazy about the way they themselves were living, because it was the only way to live.)

One night several wolves were killed in an earthquake and this was blamed on the rabbits, for it is well known that rabbits pound[1] on the ground with their hind legs and cause earthquakes. On another night one of the wolves was killed by a bolt[2] of lightning and this was also blamed on the rabbits, for it is well known that lettuce-eaters cause lightning.

The wolves threaten to civilize the rabbits if they didn't behave, and the rabbits decided to run away to a desert island. But the other animals, who lived at a great distance, shame them, saying, "You must stay where you are and be brave. This is no world for escapists[3]. If the wolves attack you, we will come to your aid[4], in all probability."

So the rabbits continued to live near the wolves and one day there was a terrible flood which drowned a great many wolves. This was blamed on the rabbits, for it is well known that carrot-nibblers[5] with long ears cause floods. The wolves descended on[6] the rabbits, for their own good, and imprisoned[7] them in a dark cave, for their own protection.

When nothing was heard about the rabbits for some weeks, the other animals demanded to know what had happened to them. The wolves replied that the rabbits had been eaten and since they had been eaten the affair was a purely internal matter.

But the other animals warned that they might possibly unite against the wolves unless some reason was given for the destruction of rabbits. So the wolves gave them one.

"They were trying to escape," said the wolves, "and, as you know, this is no world for escapists."

↗ James Thurber (1894-1961):
The Rabbits Who Caused All the Trouble

---

1. pound [paʊnd] (v.) to move, especially to run, fast or energetically and with heavy, noisy steps 腳步沉重地走 (或跑)
2. bolt [boʊlt] (n.) a flash of lightning that looks like a white line against the sky 閃電；電光
3. escapist [ɪˈskeɪpɪst] (n.) a daydreamer or fantasist who tries to avoid reality 逃避現實者
4. aid [eɪd] (n.) help or support 幫助；救援
5. nibble [ˈnɪbəl] (v.) to take a series of small quick bites at something, or eat something in a series of small quick bites 細咬；啃咬
6. descend on: to come in force 突然襲擊
7. imprison [ɪmˈprɪzən] (v.) to put in or as if in prison; confine 監禁；關押

5 Prose & Poem

The Evil Mothers (Giovanni Segantini, 1858-1899)

▌▌▌ The Depths of Heart

🎧111   In the depths of every heart, there is a tomb and a dungeon[1], though the lights, the music, and revelry[2] above may cause us to forget their existence, and the buried ones, or prisoners whom they hide. But sometimes, and oftenest at midnight, those dark receptacles[3] are flung[4] wide open.

  In an hour like this, when the mind has a passive sensibility, but no active strength; when the imagination is a mirror, imparting[5] vividness to all ideas, without the power of selecting or controlling them; then pray that your griefs may slumber[6], and the brotherhood of remorse not break their chain.

↗ Nathaniel Hawthorne (1804-1864):
The Haunted Mind

112 The Moon

The moon is a white strange world, great, white, soft-seeming globe in the night sky, and what she actually communicates to me across space I shall never fully know. But the moon that pulls the tides, and the moon that controls the menstrual[7] periods of women, and the moon that touches the lunatics[8], she is not the mere dead lump[9] of the astronomist . . . When we describe the moon as dead, we are describing the deadness in ourselves. When we find space so hideously void[10], we are describing our own unbearable emptiness.

> ↗ D. H. Lawrence (1885-1930): *Introduction to The Dragon of the Apocalypse by Frederick Carter*

1. dungeon [ˈdʌndʒən] (n.) a prison cell, often underground, especially beneath a castle 地牢；土牢
2. revelry [ˈrevəlri] (n.) noisy or unrestrained merrymaking 狂歡
3. receptacle [rɪˈseptəkəl] (n.) a container used for storing or putting objects in 貯藏所
4. fling [flɪŋ] (v.) to move or do something quickly and energetically 猛烈地開
5. impart [ɪmˈpɑːrt] (v.) to grant a share of; bestow 分給；給予
6. slumber [ˈslʌmbər] (v.) to be asleep 睡眠
7. menstrual [ˈmenstruəl] (a.) occurring during, or connected with, menstruation 每個月的；月經的
8. lunatic [ˈluːnətɪk] (n.) someone who behaves in a foolish or dangerous way 瘋子
9. lump [lʌmp] (n.) a piece of a solid substance, usually with no particular shape 一團
10. void [vɔɪd] (a.) a large empty space 空的

113 Birth

Our birth is but a sleep and a forgetting;
The soul that rises with us, our life's Star,
Hath[1] had elsewhere its setting,
And cometh from afar;
Not in entire forgetfulness,
And not in utter[2] nakedness,
But trailing[3] clouds of glory do we come
From God, who is our home:
Heaven lies about us in our infancy[4]!

↗ William Wordsworth (1770-1850):
Ode: Intimations of Immortality

1. hath [hæθ] (v.) third person singular present tense of have〔古〕= has
2. utter ['ʌtər] (a.) at the most extreme point or of the highest degree
完全的；十足的
3. trailing ['treɪlɪŋ] (a.) having a long stem which spreads over the ground
or hangs loosely 蔓生的
4. infancy ['ɪnfənsi] (n.) the time when someone is a baby or a very young
child 嬰兒期；幼年

The Pretty Baa Lambs (Ford Madox Brown, 1821-1893)

114 My Heart Leaps Up

My heart leaps up when I behold
A rainbow in the sky:
So was it when my life began;
So is it now I am a man;
So be it when I shall grow old,
Or let me die! The Child is father of the Man;
And I could wish my days to be
Bound each to each by natural piety.

↗ William Wordsworth (1770-1850)

The Door of Mercy (Arthur Hughes, 1832-1915)

115 Joy and Sorrow

The deeper that sorrow carves[1] into your being,
    the more joy you can contain.
Is not the cup that holds your wine the very cup
    that was burned in the potter's oven?
And is not the lute[2] that soothes your spirit,
    the very wood that was hollowed with knives?
When you are joyous, look deep into your heart
    and you shall find it is only that
    which has given you sorrow that is giving you joy.

When you are sorrowful look again in your heart,
and you shall see that in truth
you are weeping for that which has been your delight.
Some of you say, "Joy is greater than sorrow,"
and others say, "Nay, sorrow is the greater."
But I say unto you, they are inseparable

. . .

Verily[3] you are suspended[4] like scales[5]
between your sorrow and your joy.
Only when you are empty
are you at standstill and balanced.

↗ Kahlil Gibran (1883-1931):
The Prophet

1. carve [kɑːrv] (v.) to cut and shape a material such as wood or stone in order to make an object or design 刻
2. lute [luːt] (n.) a musical instrument which has a body with a round back and a flat top, a long neck and strings which are played with the fingers 詩琴 ; 魯特琴
3. verily [ˈverɪli] (adv.) in a completely truthful way 真實地 ; 確然地
4. suspend [səˈspend] (v.) to hang 懸掛 ; 懸浮
5. scale [skeɪl] (n.) a device on which something or somebody can be weighed 天平 ; 秤

Yesterday and Today (Kahlil Gibran, 1883-193

116 Freedom

 You shall be free indeed
  when your days are not without a care
  nor your nights without a want and a grief,
But rather when these things girdle[1] your life
  and yet you rise above them naked and unbound.
   . . .

In truth that which you call freedom
　　is the strongest of these chains,
　　though its links glitter[2] in the sun and dazzle[3] thee
　　eyes.
And what is it but fragments[4] of your own self
　　you would discard[5] that you may become free?
　　. . .
And if it is a care you would cast off,
　　that care has been chosen by you rather
　　than imposed[6] upon you.
And if it is a fear you would dispel[7],
　　the seat of that fear is in your heart
　　and not in the hand of the feared.

↗ Kahlil Gibran (1883-1931):

The Prophet

1. girdle ['gɜːrdl] (v.) to surround or encircle something 用帶子捆紮、纏繞
2. glitter ['glɪtər] (v.) to produce a lot of small bright flashes of reflected
   light 閃閃發光；閃爍
3. dazzle ['dæzəl] (v.) to make somebody temporarily unable to see
   使目眩；使眼花
4. fragment ['frægmənt] (n.) a small part broken off or detached
   碎片；片斷
5. discard [dɪsˈkɑːrd] (v.) to throw something away or get rid of it because
   you no longer want or need it 拋棄；丟棄
6. impose [ɪmˈpoʊz] (v.) to establish or apply as compulsory 把……強加於
   （impose on/upon）
7. dispel [dɪˈspel] (v.) to remove fears, doubts, and false ideas, usually by
   proving them wrong or unnecessary 消除（煩惱、恐懼等）

Now is the Pilgrim Year Fair Autumn's Charge
(John Byam Liston Shaw, 1872-1919)

117 Let Me Enjoy the Earth No Less

Let me Enjoy the earth no less
Because the all-enacting[1] Might
That fashioned forth its loveliness
Had other aims than my delight.

About my path there flits[2] a Fair,
Who throws me not a word or sign;
I'll charm me with her ignoring air,
And laud[3] the lips not meant for mine.

From manuscripts[4] of moving song
Inspired[5] by scenes and dreams unknown,
I'll pour out raptures[6] that belong
To others, as they were my own.

And some day hence, towards Paradise
And all its blest[7]—if such should be—
I'll lift glad, afar-off eyes,
Though it contains no place for me.

↗ Thomas Hardy (1840-1928)

1. enact [ɪˈnækt] (v.) to put something into action, especially to change something into a law 制定（法律）
2. flit [flɪt] (v.) to move quickly from one place to another without stopping for long 掠過
3. laud [lɑːd] (v.) to praise 讚美
4. manuscript [ˈmænjʊskrɪpt] (n.) a book or other text written by hand, especially one written before the invention of printing 手寫本；手稿
5. inspire [ɪnˈspaɪr] (v.) to make someone have a particular strong feeling or reaction 賦予……靈感
6. raptures [ˈræptʃərs] (n.) an expression of extreme pleasure and happiness or excitement （複數形）狂喜
7. blest [blest] (a.) highly favored or fortunate 幸福的；被祝福的

The Childhood of the Virgin
(Dante Gabriel Rossetti, 1828-1882)

118 Work

 You have been told also life is darkness,
and in your weariness you echo what was said by the
weary.
And I say that life is indeed darkness save when there is
urge,

And all urge is blind save when there is knowledge,
And all knowledge is vain save when there is work,
And all work is empty save when there is love;
And when you work with love
    you bind yourself to yourself,
    and to one another, and to God.

Work is love made visible.
And if you cannot work with love but only with distaste[1],
    it is better that you should leave your work
    and sit at the gate of the temple
    and take alms[2] of those who work with joy.
For if you bake bread with indifference,
    you bake a bitter bread
    that feeds but half man's hunger.
And if you grudge[3] the crushing of the grapes,
    your grudge distils[4] a poison in the wine.
And if you sing though as angels,
    and love not the singing,
    you muffle[5] man's ears
    to the voices of the day and the voices of the night.

↗ Kahlil Gibran (1883-1931): *The Prophet*

---

1. distaste [dɪsˈteɪst] (n.) a feeling of intense dislike 不喜歡；厭惡
2. alms [ɑːlmz] (n.) in former times, money or other assistance given to people in need as charity 施捨（物）; 救濟（品）
3. grudge [grʌdʒ] (v.) to be envious or resentful of somebody for something 怨恨
4. distil [dɪˈstɪl] (v.) to purify a liquid by boiling it and then condensing its vapor, or undergo purification in this way 蒸餾；提煉
5. muffle [ˈmʌfəl] (v.) to make a sound quieter and less clear 蒙住

Valkyrie and Raven (Anthony Frederick Sandys, 1829-1904)

119 The Road Not Taken

Two roads diverged[1] in a yellow wood,
And sorry I could not travel both
And be one traveler, long I stood
And looked down one as far as I could
To where it bent in the undergrowth[2];

Then took the other, as just as fair,
And having perhaps the better claim,
Because it was grassy and wanted wear;
Though as for that, the passing there

Had worn them really about the same,
And both that morning equally lay
In leaves no step had trodden black.
Oh, I kept the first for another day!
Yet knowing how way leads on to way,
I doubted if I should ever come back . . .

I shall be telling this with a sigh
Somewhere ages and ages hence:
Two roads diverged in a wood, and I—
I took the one less traveled by,
And that has made all the difference.

↗ Robert Frost (1874-1963)

1. diverge [daɪˈvɜːrdʒ] (v.) to separate and go in different directions
   （道路等）分叉；叉開
2. undergrowth [ˌʌndərˈɡroʊθ] (n.) bushes, small trees, or other vegetation
   growing beneath the trees in a forest（大樹下的）矮樹叢

120 Our Bias

The hour-glass[1] whispers to the lion's paw,
The clock-towers tell the gardens day and night,
How many errors Time has patience for,
How wrong they are in being always right.

Yet Time, however loud its chimes[2] or deep,
However fast its falling torrent[3] flows,
Has never put the lion off his leap
Nor shaken the assurance of the rose.
For they, it seems, care only for success;
While we choose words according to their sound
And judge a problem by its awkwardness[4];
And Time with us was always popular.
When have we not preferred some going round
To going straight to where we are?

↗ Wystan Hugh Auden (1907-1973)

1. hour-glass ['aʊrglæs] (n.) a time-measurement device consisting of
   two transparent bulbs connected by a narrow tube and containing an
   amount of sand that takes a specific time to flow between the bulbs
   after inversion 沙漏
2. chimes [tʃaɪmz] (n.) a set of small bells, or objects that make ringing
   sounds（複數形）鐘聲；鐘樂
3. torrent ['tɑːrənt] (n.) a fast and powerful rush of liquid, especially water
   （水、熔岩等的）奔流；洪流
4. awkwardness ['ɔːkwərdnəs] (n.) the quality of being inelegant
   粗劣；笨拙

The Hireling Shepherd (William Holman Hunt, 1827-1910)

121 What It Is To Love

Good shepherd, tell this youth what 'tis to love.
It is to be all made of sighs and tears;
. . .
It is to be all made of faith and service:
. . .
It is to be all made of fantasy,
All made of passion, and all made of wishes;
All adoration[1] duty, and observance[2],
All humbleness[3], all patience, and impatience,
All purity, all trial, all obedience[4].

↗ William Shakespeare (1564-1616):
As You Like It (Act 5 Scene 2)

122 When You Are Old

When you are old and gray and full of sleep,
And nodding by the fire, take down this book,
And slowly read, and dream of the soft look
Your eyes had once, of their shadows deep;

How many loved your moments of glad grace,
And loved your beauty with love false or true,
But one man loved the pilgrim[5] soul in you,
And loved the sorrows of your changing face;

And bending down beside the glowing bars,
Murmur[6], a little sadly, how Love fled
And paced[7] upon the mountains overhead
And hid his face amid a crowd of stars.

↗ William Butler Yeats (1865-1939)

1. adoration [ˌædəˈreɪʃən] (n.) very strong love for someone 愛慕
2. observance (n.) the execution of or compliance with laws, instructions, or customs 遵守；奉行
3. humbleness [ˈhʌmbəlnəs] (n.) the state of being modest and unimportant 畢恭畢敬；卑賤
4. obedience [əˈbiːdiəns] (n.) the act or state of yielding willingly to control by others 順從；服從
5. pilgrim [ˈpɪlɡrɪm] (n.) a religious devotee who journeys to a shrine or sacred place 朝聖者；香客
6. murmur [ˈmɜːrmər] (v.) to speak or say very quietly 私語；小聲說話
7. pace [peɪs] (v.) to walk with regular steps, often in anxiety or impatience 踱步於

TRANSLATION

Part 1 Reading Inspiration

1 Reading 讀書

　　並非所有的書都像讀者一樣魯鈍。書中的話，有可能正針對著我們的處境而說，如果我們能真正去傾聽，有所領會，那它們會比清晨和春天更有益於我們的生命，讓我們可以對事物產生新的看法。曾有多少人就是因為讀了某本書，而為自己的生命展開新的一頁。或許某本書正是為了我們而存在，為我們說明奇蹟，並帶來新的奇蹟。我們此時無法表達出的事，也許有人在別的地方已經說過了。那些讓我們困擾迷惑、不知所措的問題，智者們莫不也遇到過，比比皆是。人人各顯神通，立德立言，解決問題。

> ↗ Henry David Thoreau: *Walden*
> 亨利・大衛・梭羅：《湖濱散記》

2 Library 藏書室

　　看待你的藏書室可要小心點。你能預見自己會如何利用它嗎？想必沒有多大把握吧！可是實際問題在於，它會怎樣對待你？你來到這裡，得到的書本將會使你廣見博聞，開啟你的好奇心，把你從裡到外或是從外到裡變個模樣。

> ↗ Ralph Waldo Emerson: *Journals*
> 拉爾夫・沃爾多・愛默生：《日記》

　　我進入我的藏書室，歷代的歷史便展現在我的面前。我呼吸著原始時代的空氣，伊甸園裡玫瑰的芬芳依然繚繞不去，這時只有天下第一窩夜鶯、只有夏娃的笑顏使之產生迴蕩。我看見金字塔平地而起，我聽見亞歷山大麾下大軍的呼叫。

> ↗ Alexander Smith: *Books and Gardens*　亞歷山大・史密斯：《書籍和花園》

3 Civilization 文明

　　希臘文明——何等引人入勝。別只告訴我你們的工商企業多麼龐大；你們的組織系統、你們的自由、平等是如何廣泛；或是你們的教堂和學校、圖書館和報紙數量如何眾多，日益茁壯；而是要告訴我，你們的文明是否——這是你們給所有這些發展冠以堂而皇之的名稱——引人入勝。

> ↗ Matthew Arnold : *Civilization in the United States*
> 麥修・阿諾德：《美國文明》

4 Knowledge 知識

知識就是幸福，因為擁有知識——廣泛淵博的知識——意味著能夠分辨真實與虛假的目標、崇高的事物與卑下的事物。認識到象徵著人類進步的那些思想和作為，意味著感受到多少世紀以來人性強烈的心跳；如果一個人在這些心靈的搏動中，感受不到一種邁向天堂的奮鬥，那麼他肯定聽不到生命和諧的躍樂聲。

↗ Helen Keller: *The Story of My Life* 海倫‧凱勒：《我的一生》

5 Learning 學問

有些事情是無法立刻理解的，我們擁有的就是時間，而必須付出大量的時間才能獲知。這些再簡單不過的事情，卻要用一生的時間去了解，從生活中得到這些微不足道的新知代價極高，也是不得不留給後人的唯一資產。

↗ Ernest Hemingway (1899-1961): *Death in the Afternoon*
歐內斯特‧海明威：《午後之死》

6 Happiness 幸福

所有人類的最偉大產業就是獲得幸福。為達此目標，愛國志士和立法者們運用無比淵博的智慧，創造出了藝術，促進了科學，制定了法律，建立了模範的社會。即使是孤立無援的野蠻人，在經歷著惡劣天氣的風吹雨打和野獸的狂暴攻擊時，也沒有一刻忘記他存在的這個宏偉目標。

↗ David Hume (1711-1776) 大衛‧休姆

7 Truth 真理

我希望你做個通情並且達理的人，這樣你所到之處，都能發現善與真。如果你必須選擇，就選擇真吧，因為那最近乎現實。不斷接近現實，我的孩子：現實之中存在力量。如果建築師準備建造高樓大廈，單純的心靈絕對必要，對於農夫、牧師也是同樣必要的。

↗ Anna Wright 安娜‧賴特

8 Science and Art 科學與藝術

真理有兩種類型：一種真理照亮道路，一種真理溫暖心靈。第一種是科學，第二種是藝術。沒有藝術，科學就會毫無用處，好比水管工人手裡拿著一副高級醫用鑷子。沒有科學，藝術就會變成一堆粗製濫造的民間傳說和情感把戲。

↗ Raymond Chandler (1888-1959): *Great Thought*
雷蒙‧錢德勒：《偉大的思想》

9　Art　藝術

　　有一種目前流傳甚廣的看法，認為藝術是奢侈的，是獨占的財富，是博物館裡的玩意兒，是人們餘暇時才能沉緬玩味的東西，與日常生活無關，甚至背道而馳。這與真理相去霄壤！若要理解一幅名畫，必須良久地凝思觀看，若要理解一首奏鳴曲，必須毫不分心地聆聽許多遍。

　　沒有幾首詩能只讀一遍，全部的妙處和意蘊便畢呈無遺。真正的理解需要視覺或聽覺、感受和靈性都能集中。不過，就姑且承認偉大的藝術相對而言是珍品，真正的鑑賞是需要費神和閒趣的，但是藝術和藝術的生活方式依然充斥於我們生活的世界裡。

　　↗ Helen Louise Gardner: *Art in Everyday Life*＊
　　海倫‧路易斯‧加德納：《日常生活的藝術》

10　Music　音樂

　　確實音樂也寓於美之中，丘比特撥動的無聲音符，它的甜美遠超過樂器製造的音響。因為凡是和諧、秩序或平衡存在的地方，音樂也存在；由此說來，我們或已享受自然的天籟；因為那些井然有序的運動，那些規律的節奏，雖未把樂聲傳達耳畔，卻演奏出無比和諧的音符，讓人心領神會。

　　↗ Sir Thomas Browne＊
　　湯瑪士‧布朗爵士

　　你要知道，無情的是音樂竟如此之美。音樂具有孤獨和痛苦之美：力量和自由之美；失望和永無滿足的愛情之美；自然的無情之美，和單調的永恆之美。

　　↗ Benjamin Britten＊　班傑明‧布烈頓

11　Taste and Judgment　品味和見地

　　讀完大學卻被評為缺乏品位和見地，何以會有這樣的人？他日後會有什麼遭遇？他的下場又將是什麼？時下人們在為大學畢業生辦夜校，諸位都知道。為什麼要辦呢？因為他們受的教育不足，在當代文學園地裡摸不到門徑。在圖書館和美術館裡，他們不知該如何判斷喜愛的作品。他們不知道如何評斷一場政治運動，不知道何時會受到一個隱喻、一個類比，或一個寓言的愚弄。隱喻，正是我們要探究的論題。以詩歌教育，就是以隱喻教育。

　　試想若你我突然失去了想像力、進取心、熱情、靈感和創意——多麼可怕的字眼；試想當我們再也不重視這些特質，最起碼還有兩樣東西，我們不可掉以輕心：品味和見地。大家以為美國人見地多於品味，不過品味是要認真對待的。這也就是詩歌，藝術院校裡唯一的藝術，存在的目的。

　　我絕不怯於主張熱情。有的熱情如令人目眩的亮光，有的如震耳欲聾的呼喊，如此不修邊幅的熱情即使讀了詩也得不到教育，那就超出了詩歌的範圍。舉例說明的話，就是我可以稱之為「觀日落時嘖嘖讚嘆。」朝西觀日落，或早早起床，朝東觀日出，諸位就會嘖嘖叫好，一片此起彼落的驚嘆聲，僅此而已。

↗ Robert Frost: *Education by Poetry*
羅伯特‧佛洛斯特：《運用詩歌進行教育》

12　Time 光陰

聰明人的時間得以延長於他有思想，愚人的時間得以延長於擁有熱情。愚人的光陰是漫長的，因為他不知如何打發時光；聰明的人光陰也是漫長的，因為他用有益或有趣的想法，讓每寸光陰都更有意義。換言之，愚人希望盡快消磨時光，而聰明人總是在享受時光。

聰明人年紀增長，知識與智慧也隨之增長；愚人的年紀增長，無知與愚昧也隨之增長，他們兩者對逝去生命會有何不同的看法？後者猶如擁有一片不毛之地，滿目光禿的丘陵平原，長不出任何有益或裝飾性的東西；前者則看到一片美麗廣闊的風光，有悅目怡神的花園、綠色的牧場、豐饒的田野，目光投向任何一處，擁有的一處處總有美麗的芳草或鮮花，美不勝收。

↗ Joseph Addison: *On the Idea of Time*　約瑟夫‧艾迪生：《論時間觀念》

13　Direction 方向

我發現這世上的關鍵問題，不是我們處於何方，而是我們朝什麼方向前進：為了到達航向天堂的港口，我們勢必有時是順風航行，有時是逆風行舟──可是我們必須航行，不可漂流，也不可停泊。

↗ Oliver Wendell Holmes　奧立弗‧溫德爾‧霍姆斯

14　Courage 勇氣

勇氣有多種表現形式。有生理上的勇氣，有道德上的勇氣。然而還有品格更高一層的勇氣──這種勇氣就是勇敢面對痛苦，忍受痛苦，絕不讓他人知道痛苦，而且依然能夠在生活之中找到歡樂；清晨醒來時懷著熱情去迎接嶄新一天到來的勇氣。

↗ Howard Cosell　霍華德‧克塞爾

15　The Englishman 英國男人

我就開門見山地說吧：主宰英國男人的乃是他的心境，也就是他靈魂的晴雨，那沒什麼特別的精神或神秘成分。當他運動之後開始喝茶或啤酒，並且點燃煙斗的時候；當他在花園裡或爐火邊攤開四肢，坐在舒適的不得了的扶手椅時；當他洗刷得乾乾淨淨毅然做禮拜，面朝東方背誦使徒信經（喜歡的話還下跪）但看來絲毫不信奉其中的一字一句的時候；當他聽見或唱起最粗俗感傷又空洞的流行歌曲，卻毫不感動但並不反感的時候；當他決心選擇至交或自己喜好的詩人的時候；當他接納一方或是心上人的時候；當他打獵射擊或泛舟或大步穿行於原野的時候；當他選擇服裝或職業的時候——使他拿定主意的，從來就不是某個確切的理由或目的或外在條件，而總是他內在的心境。

⤴ George Santayana: *Soliloquies in England*　喬治・桑塔亞那：《在英國的獨白》

16　A Picture of Americans　美國人的寫照

　　這是一幅奇異而又引人入勝的美國人寫照。倘若說哪個民族有某個充滿遠大目標與夢想的傳統做後盾，那麼美國人民就具有這種傳統。在這個合眾國裡，我們沒有一個人、沒有一個孩子不知道我國的歷程。我們美洲大陸的全部歷史，就是展現我們想像力的一部歷史。

　　人們夢想著到森林、大平原、河流、山脈——而且最終也真正發現了這些平原山脈。不是恐怖的力量、不是人口的壓力迫使我們的祖先穿越這片大陸。他們是偉大的探險者，橫渡大西洋來到這裡，因為他們的頭腦具有想像力——因為他們想像著有一個更美好、更美麗、更自由、更快樂的世界；因為他們那些人不僅有勇氣、不僅有體力和吃苦耐勞的精神，而且有著熱烈活躍的渴望；因為他們有所渴望；因為他們具有渴望的活力。

⤴ Archibald MacLeish: *A Continuing Journey*
麥克李希：《持續的旅程》

17　The Native Americans　印第安人

　　印第安人的祖先，大約在三萬年前，經由亞洲穿越白令海峽，來到美洲大陸。到了哥倫布時代，定居北美洲的已有七百多個部落。這些部落迥然不同，語言、住處、宗教習慣、管理體制都不一樣。

　　印第安人以狩獵和拾荒為主，後來才漸漸開發農業，到了 1500 年，玉米已經是許多部落的重要農作物。絕大多數印第安人是愛好和平的百姓，透過談判解決分歧，而非戰爭。

⤴ Barry Bernstein: *Literature and Language*　巴里・伯恩斯坦：《文學與語言》

18　Home　家

　　家，是心所在的地方，沒有任何去處像家一樣。我對家的熱愛，不是家的外觀和地點無可比擬的。我愛家中那些無趣的用品：熱水器，滴乾餐具用的塑膠隔架，頭上的屋頂偶爾還會漏水，這些無聊的東西營造了家的氣氛——一個可靠、穩定、沒有意外、享受隱私的地方，屬於我和我的家人。家是我過生活的地方，還有什麼能要求的呢？家，就是一切。

⤴ Anna Quindlen: *Living Out Loud*
安娜・昆德蘭：《響亮的生活》

19　Supermarket　超市

　　我常去超市，這純粹是為了好玩而已，我猜想有不少人也是如此。超市填補了人們的某種需求，就像過去附近酒館所帶來的滿足感一樣。孤獨的時候，對封閉的家庭感到恐懼的時候，或是一時興起想出去融入這個繁華有趣的世界時，去超市就能夠和街坊鄰居混在一起。

　　都市的人們如今當然是深感恐懼，他們或許渴望社交生活，不過四處跟陌生人攀談是有危險的。原因有很多，其中之一便是人們已完全習慣於不與人接觸，這導致人們害怕去發現，自己其實是熱愛那種生活的。

　　不論有什麼樣的理由，人們去超市，是為了可以和別人待在一起，而非為了交談。規則似乎是，能看不能說。哦，好吧，多數的日子還是大有看頭。

↗ Russell Baker: *Small Kicks in Superland*
羅素‧貝克：《超市的小刺激》

20　People and Liberty　人民與自由

—你能愚弄所有人一時，一直愚弄部分的人，但是無法一直愚弄所有的人。

—我怕你們並未真正了解到限制人民自由的危險性。人民的自由是最必不可少的事了，政府應該做出最極致的包容，對於人民的一般權利，政府都不應該有任何一絲絲的侵犯，不容有任何的危害。

—屬於人民、由人民選出來、為了人民而存在的政府，不應從這個世界上消失。

↗ Abraham Lincoln　亞伯拉罕‧林肯

21　Hate and Nonviolence　仇恨與非暴力

—彷彿無法控制而蔓延的癌症，仇恨侵蝕人格，耗盡它最重要的協調。仇恨會破壞一個人的價值觀，使他不再客觀。它使人把美說成醜，把醜說成美，混淆真與假，混淆假與真。

—在我們這個時代，非暴力是重大政治與道德問題的解答；人需要的是透過非壓迫與非暴力的途徑，來解決壓迫與暴力的問題。在對待人類的所有衝突上，人類必需前進，改採非報仇、非侵略、非報復的途徑來解決問題，而這種途徑的基礎，就是「愛」。

—我相信，沒有攻擊性的真理和無條件的愛，終將擁有最後的發言權。這也就是為什麼即使一時受挫的正義，也比一時得勝的邪惡來得強大。

↗ Martin Luther King: *Strength to Love*
馬丁‧路德‧金恩：《愛的力量》

22　Youth　愛因斯坦致青年的信

　　哦，青年：你們可知道，你們並不是渴望無比美好自由生活的第一代？你們可知道，你們的祖先和你們的感受相同——最後卻成為煩惱和仇恨的犧牲品？

你們可知道，如果你們真能熱愛並理解世人、動物、植物還有星辰，那麼天下所有的喜悦，都會成為你們的喜悦，各種痛苦也會成為你們的痛苦，你們那些熱切的願望才能得以實現？

睜開你們的雙眼，敞開你們的心靈，伸出你們的雙手，要免遭你們的先人在歷史上如此貪婪所吸取的毒害。那麼普天之下都是你們的祖國，你們的一切付出與努力都會遍地開花，造福天下。

↗ Albert Einstein: Entry written in an album ★
亞伯特‧愛因斯坦：照片上的留字

23　Rules of Civility　禮貌守則

1. 待人接物時，一舉一動應對在場人士表示幾分尊重。
2. 在他人面前不要獨自哼唱，也不要以手指腳趾扣擊出聲。
3. 他人說話時不要說話；他人站立時不要坐著，他人駐足時不要行走。
4. 不可背對他人，尤其在說話的時候；別人讀書寫字的時候，不要碰撞書桌；不要倚靠在他人身上。
5. 不要逢迎奉承，對於不喜嬉鬧的人不要與其嬉鬧。
6. 在客人面前不要讀信、讀書或讀報；不得不然時，必須道聲失陪。他人的書信避免擅自取閱；別人寫信時也不要近看。
7. 要和顏悦色，不過遇到要事則應顯得神色莊重。
8. 別人落難不可幸災樂禍，即使是與你為敵的人。
9. 不要盯著別人的疤痕看，也不要詢問它是怎麼來的。可以私下向朋友吐露的，不要在大家面前道出。
10. 在客人面前不要用聽不懂的語言講話，而要用自己本來的語言；談吐要如有品德之人，不要像低俗的人。崇高的事情要莊重對待。
11. 先思考後才說話；咬字不要不清不楚，說起話來不要太急，要有條有理清清楚楚。
12. 別人說話的時候，要傾聽，不要打擾聽眾。如果有人言語吞吞吐吐，不要主動幫人說話，也不要加以催促；不要打斷話頭，演講結束之前不要回答。
13. 不要出於好奇去打聽別人的私事，別人在私下說話時也不要走近他們。
14. 不要承擔自己無法履行的事；但要注意言而有信。

↗ George Washington ★ 喬治‧華盛頓

24　Sayings of Benjamin Franklin　富蘭克林名言

1. 做得漂亮勝於說得漂亮。

2. 對人人都要有禮貌；要和多數人合群；要和少數人親近；要和人交友；不要與人為敵。

3. 在工作上勤於學習，你就會精通。勤勞節儉，你就會富裕。節制適度，你就會健康。凡事都有德性，你就會幸福。有了這樣的品行，至少你大有希望得到這樣的結果。

4. 激情的結束便是後悔的開始。

5. 你熱愛生命嗎？那麼就不要虛度光陰，因為光陰乃是構成生命的要素。

6. 記住，時間就是金錢。

7. 我一直認為，一個有才幹的人可能帶來了不起的改變，在人世間完成一些壯舉，只要他首先形成一個良好的計畫，而且在中斷所有可能分散他注意力的娛樂或外務之後，把執行這個計畫作為他唯一的責任和任務。

8. 二十歲時，由意志支配；三十歲時，由機智支配；四十歲時，由判斷支配。

9. 欽佩是無知的女兒。

10. 時光一去不復返。

↗ Benjamin Franklin 富蘭克林

25 Sayings of Chesterfield 切斯特菲爾德名言

1. 年輕人往往自以為聰明，如同醉漢往往自以為清醒。

2. 談到今人不要蔑視，談到古人不要崇拜。

3. 千萬不要顯得比跟你交往的人更聰明，或是更有學問。對待你的學問要像戴錶那樣，放在暗袋裡：不要只是掏出來亮亮相，炫耀你有一只錶而已。

4. 做事勿忙代表他無能力處理該事。

5. 任何矯揉造作，無論外表如何，在我看來都暗示了悟性上的瑕疵。

6. 對塵世的認識只能在塵世獲得，而不是在一間斗室裡。

7. 人生的旨趣在於欣賞；欣賞不了事物是沒有道理的；如果擁有的多而欣賞的少，那也沒有道理。

8. 俗人總是最出人頭地的，因為渴望出人頭地的那種欲望是庸俗的。

9. 一個人可能理解得了宇宙，可是從來理解不了自我；自身要比任何星星更加遙遠。

10. 世上根本沒有引不起興趣的話題；唯一可能存在的是一個不感興趣的人。

↗ Philip Dormer Stanhope, 4th Earl of Chesterfield (1694-1773)
切斯特菲爾德

26 Sayings of Samuel Johnson 賽謬爾‧約翰生名言

1. 缺乏知識的正直無力又無益，缺乏正直的知識危險而可怕。

2. 一個人讀書應該是興致使然；因為將讀書當成任務對他益處不大。

3. 知識有兩種。一種是我們本身所學的專科，另一種是我們懂得哪裡能夠找到相關的資料。
4. 人生處處是如此狀況：需要忍受的太多，能夠享受的太少。
5. 榜樣總是比規矩更加奏效。
6. 語言是思想的衣冠。
7. 放棄確定之事而尋求未定之事的人是不明智的。
8. 愛情體現愚人的聰明和聰明人的愚蠢。

↗ Dr. Samuel Johnson (1709-1784) *　賽謬爾‧約翰生

27　Sayings of Francis Bacon 培根名言

1. 一個人如果開始時事事肯定，結束時就不免產生懷疑；可是如果開始時疑團叢生，結束時就能胸有成竹。
2. 希望是一頓稱心的早餐，不過卻是一頓不足的晚餐。
3. 莫大的孤寂，就是缺乏真誠的友誼。
4. 走運時不無諸多恐懼和厭惡；失意時不無安慰和希望。走運時易於發現邪惡，可是失意時易於發現美德。
5. 倘若一個人對待陌生人能夠客客氣氣彬彬有禮，那就代表他是一位世界公民。
6. 探索真理，體現於追求之中；認識真理，體現於實踐之中；信仰真理，體現於喜好之中，這是人性至高無上的善。
7. 青年人宜於創造，而非判斷；宜於付諸行，而非好為人師；宜於創業，而非守成。
8. 一般說來，愚之於智，更能體現人生。
9. 個人命運的形塑主要掌握在自己手中。
10. 讀書讓人充實，商議讓人有把握，寫作讓人嚴謹。

↗ Francis Bacon (1561-1626) *　法蘭西斯‧培根

28　Sayings of Thomas Jefferson 湯瑪士‧傑佛遜名言

1. 今日事，今日畢。
2. 自己能夠做成之事切莫麻煩別人。
3. 錢未到手之前不要花費。
4. 不需要的東西，勿因便宜而購買；金錢來之不易。
5. 驕傲為我們帶來的損失超過飢渴和寒冷。
6. 我們無須後悔飲食太少。
7. 凡是我們樂意為之之事便不嫌麻煩。
8. 尚未發生的罪惡已經讓我們遭受莫大的痛苦。

9. 處理問題要順水推舟。

10. 生氣的時候，數到十再說話；如果非常生氣，則數到一百。

↗ Thomas Jefferson (1743-1826) [★] 湯瑪士‧傑佛遜

29　Thoughts About Life　思考人生

美好的名聲勝於昂貴的香水；你死亡的日子勝於你出世的日子。

前往喪家悼念勝於前往宴會狂歡，因為在世的人應該常常提醒自己，有朝一日我們終會迎接死亡。

悲傷勝於歡笑；它可能使你面露哀悽，卻能讓你大徹大悟。

時時刻刻渴望幸福的是傻瓜，聰明的人想到的是死亡。

有聰明的人訓斥你，勝於愚蠢的人吹捧你。

↗ Good News Bible: Ecclesiastes: 7: 1-5 [★]
《佳音版聖經》：傳道書：7：1-5

30　Warning　告誡

懶惰的人們應該從螞蟻的生活方式中引以為鑒。蟻群沒有領導者、沒有頭目、沒有統治者，可是牠們在夏天儲藏食物，為過冬做準備。懶惰的人打算閒散到什麼時候？準備什麼時間才肯起床？

「我只是小睡一會兒，」他說：「我就抱著雙手略歇片刻。」

可是在他睡覺的時候，貧窮就如同手持凶器的強盜向他襲來。

↗ Good News Bible: Proverbs: 6: 6-15 [★]
《佳音版聖經》：箴言：6:6-15

31　Money　金錢

若你愛好金錢，你將永不滿足；若你渴望富裕，你將得不到想要的一切。一切都是徒勞。越是富有，你要供養的人越多。你所獲得的全部就是「你知道自己很富有」。一個做工的人也許不能保證能否吃飽喝足，不過至少他晚上能夠睡得安穩。然而，一個富人擁有太多，結果總是提心吊膽睡不著覺。

↗ Good News Bible: Ecclesiastes: 5: 10-12 [★]
《佳音版聖經》：傳道書：5:10-12

32　Mahatma Gandhi　聖雄甘地

甘地畢生的偉大目標，就是幫助貧窮受苦的人民改善生活，並盡全力救助同胞，但絕不動用武力。他反對邪惡，無論是哪一種類。當他前去了解貧苦農場工人的生活時，數以百計的人們簇擁著他。原來是一位想要幫他們的朋友來了，在他們眼裡這可是新鮮事。當警察命令甘地離開現場時，他拒絕了，在法庭上他說明他不願服從的理由，但又請求法院判他違法並要求受罰。

這麼一個人物法官不知如何處置是好，於是便無罪釋放。這便是第一步，漸漸地在印度許多地區變成了一個重大而普遍的運動——拒絕服從非正義的法令，同時又從容接受可能給予的任何處罰。

↗ Leslie W. Leavitt: *Great Men and Women*

萊斯利‧威‧萊維特：《偉人》

33　Scientist 科學家

我並不知道我在世人眼中看來會是什麼樣子，不過在我自己看來，我彷彿只是個在海岸上玩耍的男孩，偶爾消遣一下，發現了一個比普通更光滑的卵石、或更好看的貝殼，這時刻真理的汪洋展現在我面前，而我沒有發現。

↗ Isaac Newton (1643-1727): *Memoirs of Newton*

伊薩克‧牛頓：《牛頓回憶錄》

34　Albert Einstein 艾伯特‧愛因斯坦

艾伯特成長時，學習的反應很慢，這可叫他的父母擔心了，直到九歲他才能清楚地表達意思。可是他從小就對一切存有好奇心，五歲時父親送給他一個指南針，看到艾伯特對指南針轉動興奮無比，父母都很驚訝，他一生對科學的熱愛就是由此開始的。

雖然艾伯特後來成為著名的科學家，但他卻不喜歡上學。當時的德國校規很嚴，老師個個像軍官一樣鐵面無私。艾伯特在校成績很差，因為他不愛學不感興趣的東西，只有歷史老師明白這位有主見的學生。

愛因斯坦確實是個謎。不過倘若沒有這位偉大而複雜的人物對科學界作出貢獻，我們就無法獲得今日對於時間、空間、物質、能量的理解。然而，即使是今日，我們也無法完整得知這位非凡的人物究竟為科學世界提供了些什麼。

↗ P. Z. Bradbury: *Albert Einstein*

布雷德伯里：《艾伯特‧愛因斯坦》

35　Marie Curie in the Laboratory 實驗室裡的瑪麗‧居里

在家裡，身兼妻子和母親的瑪麗為年幼的女兒洗澡、做家事。在實驗室裡，科學家瑪麗帶來了重大發現。幾年前，某位科學家已經發現，一種叫做鈾的金屬會發出一種射線，瑪麗‧居里後來將它稱之為放射線。可是這種放射線是從哪裡發出的，性質為何？這是她待解的自然界奧祕，唯有科學家才能夠理解這種追求所代表的一切。

那些實驗都是得耐著性子反反覆覆進行的。有失敗、成功；失敗的多，成功的少，然後成功又多了一點。一次、兩次、十次、二十次，她重覆著自己的實驗。一切實驗似乎都證明，在她進行觀察的礦物中存在著某種東西，某種人類一無所知的放射線。

四年之前，瑪麗用文字表達她的思想，措辭大致是這樣的：人生對於我們任何一個人來說都不容易。我們必須工作，而首先我們要相信自己。我們應該相信，我們每一個人都能夠有所作為，既然我們要發現能有所為的東西是什麼，我們就必須工作，直至成功為止。

↗ Leslie W. Leavitt: *Great Men and Women*
萊斯利‧威‧勒維特：《偉人》

36 Benjamin Franklin 班傑明‧富蘭克林

班傑明‧富蘭克林去世的時候，舉國上下空前規模的人群雲集於費城，參加他的葬禮。多才多藝的富蘭克林是一位馳名天下的出版家、發明家、政治家與作家，他出身貧寒而名利雙收，他的發跡代表著美國發展的榮景。

富蘭克林出身於波士頓一戶子女眾多的貧窮人家，因此他從小就懂得自謀生計。十二歲時他跟著從事印刷業的哥哥當學徒，十七歲時跑到費城，總算在這裡擁有了自己的印刷事業；二十四歲時他出版了《窮李察曆書》。

富蘭克林的成功，讓他得以提早擺脫俗務，獻身於公益事業、政治、科學和發明。他的成就包括創建賓夕法尼亞大學，進行重要的電力實驗，發明了雙光眼鏡、避雷針，以及富蘭克林壁爐。富蘭克林從未替自己的發明申請專利權或從中獲利，反而樂意無償貢獻出來，致力於改善人類的生活。

↗ Barry Bernstein: *Literature and Language*
巴里‧伯恩斯坦：《文學與語言》

37 Ambition 我的志願

當我還是個小男孩時，我們那個密西西比河西岸的村莊裡，小伙伴們都有個念念不忘的志向：那就是當個汽船水手。我們也有其他各種維持不久的志願，不過只是一閃而過。

比如馬戲團匆匆光臨，於是我們個個熱烈地想當個小丑；再如第一個黑人滑稽說唱團來我們村裡演出，我們又個個拼命想過那種娛樂大眾的生活；還不時有個希望：要是我們好好過活，上帝就會讓我們當上海盜。這些志向後來漸漸模糊消失，一個接著一個；可是要當汽船水手的志向一直留在我們心裡。

↗ Mark Twain (1835-1910): *Autobiography*
馬克‧吐溫：《自傳》

38 My Uncle John's Home 我叔叔約翰的家

我的叔叔約翰在密蘇里州擁有一間農場，離我們位在佛羅里達州的家有四英里遠。十二、三歲以前，我每年有一半時間是在農場度過的。我和八位堂兄弟在那兒彼此作伴的生活很快樂，因此留下的回憶也是快樂的。

我還能回想起樹林深處肅然的暮色和神祕，泥土的氣味，野花的幽香，雨水沖刷後樹葉的晶瑩，大風搖晃樹枝時水滴的落地聲，遠處傳來啄木鳥聲啪達作響，一眼瞥見竄過草地的走獸。所有景象浮上眼前，一番回味，歷歷在目。

我還能看見披上秋裝的樹林，聽見我們匆匆走過落葉時發出的沙沙聲。我還能看見一串串青紫色野葡萄，我記得那股味道和氣味。我知道野黑刺莓是什麼滋味，還有榛子的味道；我還能感覺到大風吹落時，山核桃和胡桃掉落在頭頂時的一陣陣砰響。

↗ Mark Twain (1835-1910): *Autobiography* ★　馬克‧吐溫：《自傳》

39　Adversity　逆境

我經常感到沮喪，但從未陷於絕望；我把我們的躲藏視為一種冒險經歷，既浪漫又有趣。在日記裡我對一切不足與匱乏一笑置之，從現在起下定決心要過著和一般女孩不同的生活，以後也絕不作個平凡的家庭主婦。我的動機興致勃勃，即使在危機環伺下，也得看向幽默的一面，微笑以對。

↗ Anne Frank: *The Diary of a Young Girl* ★
安妮‧法蘭克：《少女日記》

40　Growing Up　成長

不能讓他們發現我的絕望，不可讓他們看出他們所造成的創傷，我無法忍受他們的同情和善意的玩笑，那會使我尖叫得更厲害。我要是講話，人人就認為我是愛現；我不作聲的時候，他們認為我可笑；我如果回答便是無禮，我如果有個好主意便是鬼點子多，我如果累了便是偷懶，我如果比該吃的多吃了一口便是自私，愚蠢、膽怯、狡詐，什麼罪名都有。

↗ Anne Frank: *The Diary of a Young Girl* ★
安妮‧法蘭克：《少女日記》

41　A Child's Dream of a Star　孩子夢中的星星

從前有個小孩，常常到處悠閒晃蕩，想著許許多多的東西。他有個妹妹，也是個孩子，是他形影不離的小伙伴。

這兩個孩子成天對一切事物都感到驚奇。他們驚異美麗的鮮花；他們驚奇天空的高遠蔚藍；他們也對深深的清澈海水感到驚訝；上帝創造出美好的世界，他們對上帝的善良和勢力也感到驚奇。

有時他們彼此訴說著，假設天下的兒童都將死去，鮮花、大海和天空會不會因此難過？

他們相信一定會的。他們說，因為蓓蕾是鮮花的孩子，沿著山腰喧騰的頑皮小溪是大海的孩子；天空中整夜玩著捉迷藏遊戲的明亮小不點兒，肯定就是星星的孩子；要是再也看不到一起玩耍的伙伴、人類的孩子們，天地萬物都會傷心難過的。

　　有一顆清亮閃耀的明星，總是在夜空中首先露面，靠近教堂的塔尖，在墳墓的上方。他們以為，這顆星星比起所有其他的星星更大更美麗。每天晚上他們手拉手站在窗口旁，等著看明星的出現。要是先看見了，就叫喊道：「我看見那顆星星了！」

　　他們時常是兩人同時叫喊起來，什麼時候什麼方位那顆星星會升起，他們都清清楚楚。於是他們成了很要好的朋友，在床上進入夢鄉之前，他們總是往窗外再看一眼，向那顆星星道聲晚安；他們轉身入睡的時候，總要說聲「願上帝保佑星星！」

↗ Charles Dickens (1812-1870)[★] 狄更斯

42　Growing Up　成長

　　六歲那一年，大人告訴她，她現在是大女孩了。她興高采烈上學去了。大人拉住她的手，她便使勁抓住大人的那隻手，一大一小走上大樓的台階，穿過門口，來到教室的入口；然後她就得鬆手，就得面對坐滿小朋友的教室。她只認得幾個人，可是多數面孔她以前從未看過。

　　時光流逝，不覺之間到了慶祝她十歲生日的時候。她長到十三歲時更是隆重地替她慶生。

　　還有其他的大場面，十六歲是一次，然後是二十一歲：這時便是能夠投票的成人，能夠表明立場的年輕女士。每個成長階段都融入下一個階段，如此水到渠成。當然，總是會有未來在等待。學習就是生活，生活的滋味也在於學習。

↗ Elizabeth Yates (1905-2001): Always Ahead[★]
伊麗莎白・葉慈：《天天向上》

43　The Black Cat　黑貓

　　我天生稟性溫順仁慈，從幼年起就出了名。我的心腸實在太軟，大家顯而易見，也讓我成為同伴們嘲笑的對象。我特別喜愛動物，爸媽寵我，因此家裡養了各種的寵物。

　　我和牠們一起度過了大半時光，最開心不過的就數餵養和撫摸牠們的時候了。性格上的這種特點隨著我的成長而漸漸形成，在我成年後，這也是我主要的快樂來源。

　　有些人對一隻忠實且有靈性的家犬懷有一種愛憐之情，由此而來的是何等強烈的滿足，我幾乎不必費神對他們解釋這種快樂。對動物無私地奉獻情感，這份愛心有其可貴之處，能與動物息息相通，因為動物有太多機會檢驗人類不足道的友誼與脆弱的忠貞。

↗ Edgar Allan Poe (1809-1849): The Black Cat[★]
愛倫・坡：《黑貓》

303

44　Old Town in America　美國舊城

　　從前在美國中心有個城鎮，在那裡的一切生物似乎都和周圍的環境和諧相處。一間間農場縱橫交錯、繁茂興盛。城鎮正位於中心地帶，遍地糧田，山腰果樹成林，春天綠油油的田野上飄過一片片豐盛白色的雲朵。秋天橡樹、楓樹、樺樹展現耀眼的秋色，如同火焰一般閃爍不已，穿過後面的一片松林。山間可聞狐狸叫，小鹿靜靜地走過一片片田野，隱沒在秋日清晨的薄霧中。

↗ Rachel Carson (1907-1964): *Silent Spring* ★
瑞秋・卡森：《寂靜的春天》

45　The Way to Rainy Mountain　雨山之路

　　一座小圓丘在奧克拉荷馬的大平原上兀然隆起，位於威奇托山脈的西北方。在奇歐瓦族人眼中，這座圓丘是個古老的地標，為其取名為雨山。

　　那裡有天下最險惡的氣候，冬日暴風雪來臨，酷熱的龍捲風竟在春天刮起，夏天大平原就像鋼砧的邊緣，青草變得脆硬枯黃，腳踩時發出霹啪霹啪的聲音。沿著河流溪澗是綠色的狹長地帶，山核桃和大胡桃樹、柳樹和金縷梅，形成一條線道的樹叢。七八月裡往遠處望去，冒著熱氣的樹葉彷彿在大火中扭曲。黃綠色的大蚱蜢在高高的草叢裡舉目皆是，如同玉米似的突地冒出刺痛皮膚，烏龜在紅土上四處爬行，好半天也沒爬多遠。

　　孤寂是這片土地的特色。平原上萬物都是形單影隻的；視線裡景物不會紛然雜呈，只有一座小山、一棵樹或是一個人。一大清早觀望那裡的風光，分不清前後遠近，因為朝陽還在你的背後。此時想像力開始活躍，你會聯想到，這裡就是天地萬物被創造的地方。

↗ N. Scott Momaday (1934-): *The Way to Rainy Mountain* ★
恩・司考特・蒙馬戴：《雨山之路》

46　Long Journey for School　漫漫求學路

　　經過好幾天的路程，一邊行走，一邊懇求別人讓我搭乘馬車和汽車，我到達了維吉尼亞州首府里奇蒙，與漢普頓相距大約八十二哩。我到達那裡的時候，又累、又餓、又髒，已經是深夜了。我從沒在大城市裡待過，這使我的處境加倍艱難。抵達里奇蒙時，我已身無分文。我在那兒一個熟人都沒有，城市道路我不熟悉，實在不知道該去哪裡。我到了幾處地方去投宿，可是它們全都要收錢，而我所缺的正是錢。

　　不知所措的時候，我只好流浪街頭。這時候我路過好些個賣吃的路邊攤，炸雞和半月形的蘋果餡餅堆得高高的，令人垂涎三尺。

那個時候在我看來，我有可能期望未來擁有的一切，就是抓住一隻雞腿或是一個餡餅。可是兩樣東西我一樣也得不到，也沒有任何其他可吃的東西。

↗ Booker T. Washington (1856-1915): *Up From Slavery* ★
布克·華盛頓：《超越奴役》

47　We Travel Towards the Moon　月球之行

我們睡覺、看書、玩遊戲，打發時間。我透過無線電和地球上的父母說話，他們很擔心，說從報紙上看到了事故的消息。我讓他們別擔心，當我們離月球越來越近，我從窗口往外看；我可以看見小城、山川和空曠的田野，數以千里延綿不斷。

能夠看見月球的另一面真令人興奮，這是我們從地球上無法看見的那一面。我看不到地球了，這還是頭一回，是種奇怪的感覺。我只能看到太陽、月球和星星。

↗ Arthur C. Clarke (1917-2008): *Islands in the Sky* ★
亞瑟·克拉克：《空中島嶼》

48　The Very Proper Gander　非常正派的鵝

不久以前，有一隻出色的雄鵝，他雄赳赳的，羽毛光滑，相貌堂堂，成天對著妻兒唱歌。

有一天，有個人看見他在自家院子裡趾高氣揚來回踏步，歌聲不斷，說了一句：「有一隻正派的鵝。」

一隻老母雞無意中聽到這句話，當晚便在雞棚裡告訴老伴說：「他們不知在搞什麼名堂。」

公雞接口道：「我早就懷疑他了。」隔天，公雞在穀場四處閒晃，逢人便說那隻愛炫耀的鵝是個危險的傢伙，可能比披著鵝毛的老鷹還危險。

於是一隻棕色的小母雞想起來，有一次她老遠就看見雄鵝在樹林裡和一些老鷹交談。「他們想必是要做什麼壞事。」她說。

這時又有一隻鴨子想起來，雄鵝曾經說過他什麼都不信。「他說，什麼國旗我也不甩。」鴨子說。

一隻珍珠雞也回想起，她曾經見過有個很像雄鵝身影在扔炸彈之類的東西。

最後，大家全都拿起棍棒石塊，跑去攻擊雄鵝的住處，當時雄鵝正在前院昂首闊步，對著妻兒唱歌。

「他在那裡！」大家叫喊道：「喜愛老鷹的傢伙！沒有信仰的傢伙！憎恨國旗的傢伙！扔炸彈的傢伙！」於是他們群起攻之，把雄鵝攆出了這個國家。

↗ James Thurber (1894-1961): *Fables for Our Time* ★
詹姆斯·瑟伯：《當代寓言》

49 A Fable 寓言

　　古代的聖賢好心地發明了一種方式，可以向人們講真話而又不致於當面冒犯：他們在人們面前立起一面獨一無二的鏡子，從中看得見形形色色的動物和稀奇古怪的事情，而且這面鏡子產生了寓教於樂的奇觀。他們把它稱為「寓言」。無論動物在故事裡做了什麼愚蠢或聰明的事情，芸芸眾生都會反躬自問，而認為：寓言是暗指你們大家的。

↗ Hans Christian Andersen (1805-1875): *Andersen's Fairy Tales*

漢斯‧克里斯蒂‧安徒生：《安徒生童話集》

50 A Grain of Sand 一粒細沙

　　從一粒沙看世界，
　　從一朵花見天堂，
　　掌握無窮於掌心，
　　掌握永恆於剎那。

↗ William Blake (1757-1827)　威廉‧布雷克

51 I Wandered Lonely as a Cloud 我獨自漫遊猶如一朵飄雲

　　我獨自漫遊猶如一朵飄雲，
　　高高飄蕩在溪谷和山崗上，
　　兀然間我看見，
　　好大一片的金黃色水仙花；
　　在湖畔邊樹叢下，
　　臨風婆娑翩翩起舞。

↗ William Wordsworth (1770-1850)

威廉‧渥茲華斯

52 Nature 自然

　　在荒蕪路徑的樹林裡有樂趣，
　　在人跡罕至的河岸上有狂喜，
　　在無人的大海邊，有自然與心靈的交流，
　　奏出海浪狂嘯的樂音。
　　我雖然熱愛人類，對自然更是情有獨鍾，
　　從我們和自然的交流之中，從我的一切可能變化，
　　或是從過去的自我之中，我悄悄
　　和天地萬物交融相通，
　　感受到了我永遠無法表達無從掩飾的一切。

↗ George Gordon Byron (1788-1824): *Childe Harold's Pilgrimage*

喬治·戈登·拜倫：《哈羅德遊記》

53　Happiness 幸福

它在我心中，我不知道它是什麼，可是我知道它在我心中。

磨難淌汗──我的身體隨後漸漸平靜涼爽。

我睡了──我睡了很久。

我不知道它，它沒有名稱，它是個說不出口的字眼，

它不存在於字典、話語、符號之中……

哦，我的兄弟姐妹們，你們看到了嗎？

它不是混沌亦非死亡──它是種形式、是一種和諧、是一項計畫──

它是永恆的生命──它，就是幸福。

↗ Walt Whitman (1819-1892): *Leaves of Grass*　華特·惠特曼：《草葉集》

54　If I Can Stop One Heart from Breaking
如果我能阻止一顆心不破碎

如果我能阻止一顆心不破碎

我就不會虛度生命；

如果我能解除一個生命的病痛，

或是減緩一分疼痛，

或是幫助一隻昏厥的知更鳥

回到牠的鳥窩

我就不會虛度生命。

↗ Emily Dickinson (1830-1886)　愛蜜莉·狄更生

55　A Birthday Poem (for Rachel) 生日贈詩（給雷契爾）

我們在你生命中的每一年，

在你生日蛋糕上點燃蠟燭，

紀錄下生命中單純的進程，

這是人人都會經歷的過程，

繼而，為了考驗你的膽量

或對死亡能有適當的認識，

每年你都要吹熄每枝蠟燭，

透過你生命的氣息來吹滅。

↗ James Simmons (1933–2001)　詹姆斯·西蒙斯

56　Dreams　夢想

要牢牢守著夢想，
因為夢想倘若死亡，
生命便是一隻折翼的鳥兒，
再也無法飛翔。

要牢牢守著夢想，
因為夢想消逝的時候，
生命便是一片不毛之地，
天寒地凍，嚴雪覆蓋。

↗ Langston Hughes (1902-1967)　蘭斯頓・休斯

57　Who Has Seen the Wind?　何人看見風？

何人看見風？
不是我，也不是你；
當樹葉搖曳時，
風飄然拂過。

何人看見風？
不是你，也不是我；
當樹枝低垂時，
風飄然拂過。

↗ Christina Rossetti (1830-1894)　克莉思蒂娜・羅塞蒂

58　The Daisies　雛菊

在芬芳欲放的晨曦中——哦，
臨風的青草波瀾起伏，
我看見心愛的人悠然獨步，
在那遍地雛菊的田野間。

我倆無語無笑
幸福地四處漫遊著；
我吻著愛人的雙頰，
在芬芳欲放的晨曦中——哦，

雲雀鳴唱，來自微風吹拂的大地
雲雀鳴唱，來自遠處的一片雲，
她和我手牽著手漫步
在那遍地雛菊的田野間。

↗ James Stephens (1882-1950)[★] 詹姆斯‧史蒂芬斯

59　To— 給———

當輕柔的聲音消失，
樂聲仍迴蕩在記憶——
當甜美的紫羅蘭枯萎，
芬芳仍在感官中縈繞不去。
當玫瑰花凋零時，
花瓣仍堆在愛人的床頭；
當你棄我而去時，
你的思緒也會隨著愛情而睡去。

↗ Percy Bysshe Shelley (1792-1822)[★] 雪萊

60　The Love Song of J. Alfred Prufrock
阿爾弗瑞德‧普魯弗洛克的情歌

我漸漸老去……漸漸老去……
我將會穿著捲起褲腳的褲子。

我應該把頭髮往後分嗎？我敢吃桃子嗎？
我會穿條白色法蘭絨長褲，在海灘上漫步。
我已經聽過人魚互相高歌了。

我想牠們不會對著我高歌。

我已經看過牠們向著大海乘浪而去
梳著拂逆而來的白色浪髮
當風把海水吹得陣陣白浪黑濤。

我們一直逗留在大海幽閉的空間裡
海妖們用紅色和褐色海草做成的花環來裝飾
一旦我們被人聲喚醒，我們就會淹沒其中。

↗ T.S. Eliot (1888-1965)[★] 艾略特

61 Declaration of Independence 獨立宣言

我們認為以下的真理是不言而喻的：人人生而平等，上帝賦予每個人一些不可剝奪的權力，包括生命、自由和追求幸福的權力。

政府的成立乃是為了保障這些權力，政權則由人民授權而來。

對於無法保障這些權力的政府，人民有權改變或廢除，進而建立新政府，並採取此原則為基礎，以此方式組織權力，因為這是最可能實現安全與幸福的方法。

↗ Thomas Jefferson (1743-1826)
美國第三屆總統湯瑪斯·傑弗遜（1776 年發表）

62 The Four Freedoms 四大自由

在我們力求安定的未來日子裡，我們期待一個以人類四大基本自由為基礎的世界。

第一，世界各地都有言論與表達的自由。

第二，世界各地人人都有用自己的方式來崇拜上帝的自由。

第三，有免於匱乏的自由，用世俗的話來說，亦即在經濟上保障世界各國的居民都能夠擁有健康和平的生活。

第四，有免於恐懼的自由，用世俗的話來說，亦即徹底的世界性裁減軍備，以至於世界上任何地方的任何國家，都無法侵犯任何鄰國。

↗ Franklin D. Roosevelt (1882-1945): January 6, 1941, one of annual messages to Congress 美國第三十二屆總統羅斯福：1941 年 1 月 6 日致國會咨文

63 American Dream 美國夢

朋友們，我今天要對你們說，儘管眼前橫阻著困難和挫折，但我仍然有一個夢想。這是一個深植於「美國夢」的夢想。

我有一個夢想：將來有一天，這個國家會站起來，實踐其信條的真諦：「我們認為這些真理是不言而喻的：人人生而平等。」

我有一個夢想：將來有一天，在喬治亞州的紅土山丘上，前奴隸的孩子和前奴隸主的孩子，能夠情同手足地同坐一堂。

我有一個夢想：將來有一天，甚至在密西西比州，備受不公平與壓迫所煎熬的州郡，能夠改造成一片自由又公平的綠洲。

我有一個夢想：將來有一天，我的四個小孩所住的國家，是以品性而非膚色來評斷人的。我今天有這麼一個夢想！

我有一個夢想：阿拉巴馬州州長現在口口聲聲說干預和廢除，將來有一天，這個州能夠變成這種情況：黑人小男孩和小女孩，能夠和白人小男孩及小女孩攜手同行，如同兄弟姐妹。我今天有這麼一個夢想！

我有一個夢想：將來有一天，每個山谷都能被填平，每座山岳丘陵都能被剷平，崎嶇之處變為平原，彎處變直，上帝的光芒得以展露，眾生一同目睹。

這就是我們的希望。這就是我重返南方所抱持的信念。有了這個信念，我們就能夠在絕望之山挖掘出一塊希望之石。有了這個信念，我們就可以把國家的嘈雜不諧之音，變成一首歌頌手足之情的美妙交響曲。有了這個信念，我們就能夠一道工作，一同祈禱，共同奮鬥，一起入獄，並肩捍衛自由，明白我們總有一天終會自由。

↗ Martin Luther King (1929-1968): *I Have a Dream*
美國黑人民權領袖馬丁·路德·金：〈我有一個夢想〉

64　Inaugural Address　就職演講

在漫長的世界史上，只有幾代人在自由臨危之際，能夠被允許去捍衛自由。

我不會逃避這種責任——我樂而接受。我想，我們當中沒有人願意和其他任何民族或世代的人交換身分。我們為此一努力所付出的精力、信念和奉獻，將照亮我們的國家和所有為國效力的人——而這把火的光輝也能夠真正照亮全世界。

因此，我的美國同胞們：不要問國家可以為你做些什麼，而是問你自己能為國家做些什麼。

我的世界公民同胞們：不要問美國能為你們做些什麼，而是問我們能夠共同為人類的自由做些什麼。

最後，不論諸位是美國公民還是世界公民，在此要求我們能夠堅強和犧牲，而那正是我們彼此所要求的。我們要求你們心安理得，心安理得是我們唯一確定的報償，歷史是我們行為的最後審判者，且讓我們去領導我們所熱愛的國家，祈求上帝的祝福與幫助。我們要明白，在這塵世上，我們要真正把上帝的工作當成我們自己的工作。

↗ John Fitzgerald Kennedy (1917-1963)
美國第三十五屆總統甘迺迪的就職演說

65　I Hear America Singing　我聽見美利堅在歌唱

我聽見美利堅在歌唱，我聽見各種歡唱，
技工的歡唱，各自唱著自己的歌，快活又健壯，
木匠在量木板或橫梁時，唱著自己的歌，
水泥匠準備上工或歇工時，唱著自己的歌，

船夫歌唱船上所有的一切，甲板水手在輪船甲板上歌唱，

鞋匠坐在長凳上歌唱，帽匠站著歌唱，

樵夫之歌，莊稼漢在早晨上工、中午休息和太陽西下時歌唱，

母親、工作中的年輕妻子、縫洗衣服的女孩，她們歌聲甜潤，

人人都唱著只屬於自己的歌曲。

白天唱著白天的事──夜裡，健康友善的成群年輕人，

大唱他們雄壯而優美的歌。

↗ Walt Whitman (1819-1892): Leaves of Grass
美國詩人惠特曼：《草葉集》

66　New York　紐約

一首詩壓縮在小小篇幅裡，加進音樂感，平添了意味。紐約市宛如詩歌韻文：它把所有的生活和各種族各類型的人，都壓縮在一個小島上，並且添進了樂感和內燃機的伴奏。曼哈頓毫無疑問是世界上最大的人類縮影之地，千百萬永久居民領略這首詩的魔力，但詩的全部意味永遠撲朔迷離。

在最高聳最豪華的辦公樓底下，是最骯髒破舊的貧民窟。河畔教堂內儲藏的風雅神秘之物，和哈林區的巫毒符咒只隔著幾個街區。商界鉅子坐在黑頭車上，沿著東河大道駛向華爾街，離個幾百碼和吉普賽王交錯而過卻渾然不知。那些吉普賽王還沒有起床呢，比起商業鉅子，他們的生活更加悠哉，更常一醉方休。

↗ E. B. White (1899-1985): Here Is New York
美國作家懷特：《這就是紐約》

67　Nostalgia　鄉愁

心裡頭有一種鄉愁，那是一種奇特的情感。對美國人來說，這是一種民族特性，就像雲霄飛車或投幣點唱機那樣為我們所特有。鄉愁，不單是指思念故鄉或出生地。這種情感有著兩種臉孔，一種是對熟悉事物的懷舊，另一種是渴望異域和陌生的衝動，我們夾在中間受其折騰。而最令我們懷起鄉愁的地方，往往是我們一無所知的地方。

↗ Carson McCullers (1917-1967): Look Homeward, Americans
美國女作家卡森·麥卡勒斯：《望鄉，美國人》

68　England and the English　英格蘭與英國人

你會發現，英國人所做的事，非極壞，則極好，但你就是不會發現他們理虧。他們做什麼事都是有原則的，和你打仗時，他們根據愛國原則；搶劫你的時候，根據商業原則；奴役你的時候，根據帝國主義原則；欺負你的時候，根

據男子漢原則；支持皇室，是根據忠誠原則；把國王的頭砍掉，則是依據共和體制原則。他的口號都是責任，而且他也忘記過，讓責任變得違背利益的那個國家已經消失。

↗ George Bernard Shaw (1856-1950): The Man of Destiny
愛爾蘭劇作家、小說家及評論家蕭伯納：《人的命運》

69　Westminster Abbey　西敏寺

看著偉人之墓，我不再有妒忌之情；讀著紅粉佳人的墓誌銘，縱情之慾煙消雲散；看見墓石上的悲痛父母，我內心一陣憐憫；看見雙親之墳，想到我們也將隨之而去，便覺憂傷無益；看到國王和罷黜自己的人躺在一起，想到互相敵對的人並肩而臥，想到爭論不休而讓世界分裂的僧侶，人類那種雞毛蒜皮的競爭、內訌和爭辯，就讓我感到悲哀與驚訝。讀到墓上的一些日期，有些死於昨天，有些死於六百年前，我想在審判日那一天，我們都會變成同時代的人，一齊出現。

↗ Joseph Addison (1672-1719): Spectator (No. 26)
英國政治家及散文作家約翰‧艾迪生：《旁觀者》第 26 期

70　French Revolution　法國大革命

這是最好的時代，也是最壞的時代；那是智慧的年代，也是愚蠢的年代；那是信仰的紀元，也是懷疑的紀元；那是光明的時刻，也是黑暗的時刻；那是希望的春天，也是絕望的冬天；我們眼前擁有一切，我們眼前也一無所有；我們都直接走向天堂，也直接走向另一端——總之，那個時期如同現在一樣，喧嚷的權威人士，要求人們必須接受它，無論把它當作最好，還是把它當作最壞。

↗ Charles Dickens (1818-1870): A Tale of Two Cities
英國小說家狄更斯：《雙城記》

71　The Battle of Waterloo　滑鐵盧之戰

那一天，從早晨到日落炮聲隆隆，沒有停過。天黑之後，炮轟才突然停止。

我們都讀到過當時發生了什麼事，每個英國人都講著這個故事。大戰決定勝負的時候，我你都還是小孩子，我們聽了又聽，講了又講，對這場名役一點也不會感到厭倦。

那些當天戰敗的百萬勇敢同胞，他們想起這件事時仍是忿恨難平，巴不得有機會雪恥。如果戰後的勝利站在他們那邊，他們成了得意的一方，把可怕的仇恨和憤怒留給我們，兩個不甘示弱的國家就會沒完沒了地鬥下去。光榮與恥辱，殺敵成功或不成，互相消長，沒有終止。

數百年後，我們法國人和英國人可能還在互相吹噓和殘殺，勇敢地維護魔鬼的「榮譽」法典。

↗ William Makepeace Thackeray (1811-1863): Vanity Fair
英國小說家薩克雷:《名利場》

72　Walt Whitman　沃爾特・惠特曼

　　沃爾特・惠特曼對於藝術的摒棄,讓他成了個藝術家。他嘗試用特定的手法來產生特定的效果,他是做到了⋯⋯。他特立獨行,他的作品的主要價值在於其預言性,而非文字工夫。他開始了恢宏主題的序曲,他是新紀元的先驅。就人來說,他是新人種的先輩,是人類那英雄般的精神演化的代理人。倘若詩歌遺漏了他,哲學總會注意到他。

↗ Oscar Wilde (1854-1900): Review of Whitman
愛爾蘭劇作家、詩人、小說家及評論家王爾德:〈評惠特曼〉

73　William Shakespeare　莎士比亞

　　看到羅密歐和茱麗葉,我們自己成了戀人,看到哈姆雷特,我們成了學子。鄧肯的鮮血在我們的雙手裡流淌著,我們和泰蒙一起憤世嫉俗,李爾王在荒原遊蕩時,瘋狂的恐懼觸動了我們。我們既有黛絲狄蒙娜的清白,也有以阿苟的罪孽。

↗ Oscar Wilde (1854-1900): The Portrait of Mr. W. H.
愛爾蘭劇作家、詩人、小說家及評論家王爾德:《威・赫先生的畫像》

74　Three Passions　三種激情

　　有三種簡單卻無法遏止的激情,主宰了我的生活:對愛的渴望,對知識的追求,以及對人類苦難所懷的難忍憐憫。這些激情,猶如狂風,吹得我忽東忽西,行跡不定,飄過深沈的苦海,來到絕望的邊緣。

　　我追求愛,首先是因為它帶來狂喜——莫大的狂喜,我常會為了幾個鐘頭的這種喜悅,而把生活的其他部分都犧牲掉。我追求愛,再者是因為它能夠排解寂寞——那種可怕的寂寞,陷入其中,打著哆嗦的知覺會處在世界的邊緣之上,看到冰冷、深不可測、毫無生息的深淵。我追求愛,最後是因為在愛的結合之中,在神秘的縮影裡,我看到了聖賢和詩人所想像和預示出的天堂。這就是我所追求的,儘管看似超乎人生的美好,但這就是我「最終」的發現。

　　懷著同樣的激情,我追求知識。我希望能夠認識人類的心靈,想知道星星為什麼會發光,努力了解「數字」支配流變的畢達哥拉斯力量。我在這方面小有所成,但不太多。

　　愛與知識,在可能的情況下,引人向上通往天堂,然而,憐憫總是把我帶回塵世。痛苦的哭泣聲在我心裡迴盪,飢餓的兒童,受壓迫者所折磨的苦難者,成為子女所痛恨的像包袱一樣的無助老人，充滿孤獨、貧困和痛苦的整個世界，嘲諷著人生的應有面貌。我渴望減緩不幸，但我無能為力，我也受著苦。

這就是我的生命。我發現它值得生活下去，如果有機會，我樂意再活一次。

↗ Bertrand Russell (1872-1970): Autobiography

英國哲學家羅素：《自傳》

75　Life Worth Living　生活值得活下去

我出身於工人階級。我早年就發現了熱忱、抱負和理想這種東西，要去滿足它們，便成了我童年生活的難題。我的環境粗糙、簡陋又粗鄙，我沒有什麼「前」景可言，倒不如說是只能向「上」看。我處在社會的底層，那裡的生活無論是在身體或心靈上，都只有卑下悽慘可言，身心兩者同樣饑渴與備受磨折。

我頭上聳立著社會這座雄偉的驚人建築物，對我來說，唯一的出路就是「往上」。我很早就下定決心要爬進這座大建築物。在上面，男人穿的是黑色制服和襯衫，婦女穿的是炫爛的禮服，而且有著又棒又多的東西可以吃。對身體來說，這已經足夠了，但那裡還有心靈所需要的東西。我知道，在那上面是無私的心靈、純潔高尚的思想和敏銳的精神生活。

我之所以知道這些，是因為我讀過「海濱書社」的小說，除了惡棍和女投機者之外，其中所描寫的男男女女，莫不思想美好、言談優雅、行為高尚。簡單說來，如同我相信太陽會昇起一樣，我相信在我之上的一切都是美好、高尚、優雅的，會讓生活變得高貴有尊嚴，足以犒賞人的痛苦與悲慘，讓生活值得活下去。

↗ Jack London (1876-1916): What Life Means to Me

美國作家傑克‧倫敦：《生活對我意味著什麼》

76　Past Love　舊愛

想起我心儀的人，我不必感到臉紅。我的戀情是告吹了，但對於自己曾經有過那麼純潔高尚的情感，我頗引以為傲。蘇珊‧柯考德小姐的美德與才華，讓她更添魅力。……

聽到有這樣一位佳人，我感到很好奇。結果我一見傾心。……

經過一番痛苦的掙扎，我向命運屈服：我嘆息如戀人，服從如兒子。時光流逝，她不在旁邊，我有了新的生活習慣，不知不覺地，時間治癒了我的傷口。我聽到可靠的消息，說她過得很平靜快樂，這讓我的恢復快了些，我的愛情也在友誼和尊敬中平息了下來。

↗ Edward Gibbon (1737-1794): Autobiography

英國歷史學家愛德‧吉本：《自傳》

315

77 Highest Reality 最高的真實

　　如果迎接金烏玉兔時莫不充滿喜悅，如果生活清芬可挹，猶如花草芳菲，如果生命更有彈性，更加燦爛不朽這便是你的成功。大自然的一切都會為你慶賀，你也能時時為自己祝福。

　　人們有眼不識最大的收穫和價值，我們很容易就懷疑它們是否真的存在，很容易就忘掉它們，但它們卻是最高的真實。最驚人、最真實的事實，或許從未被人們傳達過。

　　我一天生活的真正收穫，如晨暮之際的天色，無形而不可名狀。我所抓住的，是一點星塵，一截彩虹。

↗ Henry D. Thoreau (1817-1862): Walden
美國作家及思想家亨利・梭羅：《湖濱散記》

78 Be Lost 迷路

　　在日常的行走中，我們像領航員一樣，不知不覺地沿著某些熟悉的燈塔和岬角前進，就算偏離了平常的航道，腦海裡也都還記得某個鄰近的海岬。除非我們完全迷了路，或是轉了向——在這個世界上，一個人只需閉眼轉個向，就會迷路，然後才能欣賞到大自然的遼闊與不可思議。人從睡眠或失神中醒過來之後，常常需要再度去熟悉羅盤上的方位。

　　只有當我們迷了路——亦即當我們失去了這個世界，我們才能開始去找到我們自己，了解自己身置何處，了解自己和大自然之間的無限關係。

↗ Henry D. Thoreau (1817-1862): Walden
亨利・梭羅：《湖濱散記》

79 Flints' Pond 弗林特池

　　他只想到池子的金錢價值，他的出現是整個池岸的災難。他耗盡了周圍的土地，也樂於抽光池子裡的水。他只恨這裡不是英國的乾草地或小紅莓草坪，在他的眼裡，這個池子無可救藥，池底的淤泥要是能賣錢，他寧可抽乾池水。池水又不能轉動水磨，他也不覺得凝視池子是一件殊榮。我並不敬重他的勞動，在他的農場裡，什麼東西都有標價，要是有利可圖，他會把風景、把他的上帝帶到市場上去。他去市場，就像去膜拜他的上帝一樣。在他的農場上，沒有東西是自由生長的，他的田地沒有收成，他的牧場不開出花朵，他的樹木不結果實，它們只生產鈔票。他不愛果實的美麗，只有當果子換成銀子時，他才會覺得果子成熟了。

↗ Henry D. Thoreau (1817-1862): Walden
美國作家及思想家亨利・梭羅：《湖濱散記》

80　The Problem of Mankind　人類的問題

　　我們必須熱切不倦地努力，以拉近科學與道德在進步上的巨大差距。苦於心靈的貧瘠，是我們人類的一大問題，這與科技的豐足形成了觸目驚心的對照。我們在物質上愈是富足，我們在道德和精神上就愈是貧乏。

　　人人都活在內在與外在這兩大領域之中。內在領域即精神領域，以藝術、文學、道德、宗教的方式來呈現。外在領域由我們賴以生存的設備、工藝、機械和工具所組成。

　　我們當今的問題在於，我們聽任內在領域迷失在外在領域之中，聽任生存的手段遠遠超前於生存的目的。現代生活在諸多方面，都可援用梭羅那句啟發性的警言來做結論：「改善了方法，卻未能改善目標。」這就是現代人所遭遇到的一個重大困境，一個嚴重麻煩的問題。

　　如果心靈沒有跟著一起成長，那麼物質力量愈大，所招致的危險也就愈大。一旦人性中的外在力量勝過了內在力量，烏雲暴雨便會開始形成。

↗ Martin Luther King (1929-1968):
Where Do We Go From Here: Chaos or Community?
美國黑人民權領袖馬丁‧路德‧金：《我們從這裡走向何方：混亂還是社區？》

81　Social Problems　社會問題

　　這些是今日和我們息息相關的問題：防止戰爭；保護環境；人口與資源的平衡；資源管理，以免因人口激增而耗盡資源或污染環境；國家團體之間的資源分配，它們過去由於自然和歷史因素而分配不均；科技的人性化，使科技能應用在人性化的目的上，而非只用於利益或權力之上；重新規劃鄉鎮和都市，讓鄰里之間能夠再度成為一個三代同堂、生活完整的小天地；創造超越性的價值觀念，使得某個宗教信仰或是某個思想體系的人不再敵視異己，人們也就都無需為新棄舊。在這些問題當中，就我看來，唯有預防戰爭的需要始終明確不變。

　　或許最重要的是，我當年就毫不懷疑世界正在改變，其改變無處不在，絕對必要而無可阻擋。我認為這是生活品質的一部分，亦即，人們應該有機會去學會珍惜過去，學習在此時此刻就行動，並且留給未來開放的空間。

↗ Margaret Mead (1901-1978): Reflections on the Human Condition
↗ 美國人類學家瑪格麗特‧米德：《關於人類狀況的感想》

82　The Twentieth Century　二十世紀

　　理性與噩夢的緊密結合，主宰著二十世紀，誕生出了一個含糊多義的世界。在傳媒構成的景觀上，遊走著不幸的科技幽靈，以及金錢可以買得到的夢想。

在廣告與偽造事件、科學與色情所統治而有著強光照明的領土上，同時存在著熱核武器系統和飲料的商業廣告。操縱我們的生活的，乃是二十世紀的雙重主題──性與狂想。

↗ James Graham Ballard (1930-2009): Introduction, 1974, to the French edition of Crash
小說家巴拉德：法文版《垮台》前言，1974

83 Modern Man 現代人

一個現代人若是敢把自己對天堂的想法清楚地講出來，那他會描繪出一座天底下最大的百貨公司，裡面展示著新奇的用品和玩意，他自己有的是錢去購買。在小玩意和商品琳琅滿目的天堂裡，他逛得目瞪口呆，只要一直有更多更新的東西可以買，或許街坊就不會差他太多。

↗ Erich Fromm (1900-1980): The Sane Society
德國精神分析學家及社會哲學家弗洛姆：《健全的社會》

84 Cities and City Life 都市與都市生活

生活在都市裡頭是一門藝術，我們需要藝術和時尚的詞彙，才能在不斷創新風貌的都市生活中，描述人類與物質之間的獨特關係。於是我們想像的都市，充滿了柔性的幻想、神話和夢魘。這樣的城市，比起可按統計值繪製在地圖上，可在都市社會學、人口學、建築學專著中見到的那種生硬城市，都是同樣真實的，甚或更加真實。

↗ Jonathan Raban (b. 1942): Soft City
英國作家喬納森‧拉班：《柔性城市》

85 Poverty and the Poor 貧窮與窮人

我們變得害怕清貧了。那種為了簡化和拯救內在而甘於清貧的人，我們看不起。如果某人不加入一般人的爭奪，或是不汲汲於生財之道，我們就會認為他精神委靡，缺乏抱負。

↗ William James (1842-1910): The Varieties of Religious Experience
美國哲學家及心理學家威廉‧詹姆斯：《宗教經驗的種種》

86 Universe 宇宙

就我們目前所觀察到的來說，宇宙乃是一座奇妙巨大的發動機，它的寬廣、秩序、美麗或殘酷，處處令人嘆服。如果我們把它的生命戲劇化，構想出它的精神，我們會充滿驚訝、恐懼和興味，因為那種精神如此宏偉、豐富、不可動搖、嚴密和隱晦。就像所有的動植物一樣，宇宙有自己的行事之道，那並不全然合理或理想化，而是堅忍、不可逆且具有成效。這個由土和火所形成的有機體，何其偉大；這個巨大、艱苦、輝煌的實驗，又何其令人敬畏。

我們何不帶著虔敬心觀看宇宙？難道它不是我們的本質？難道我們是由別的塵土所構成？我們永恆的可能性就藏在其中，我們所有的喜悅都是由它所給予。

我們無需帶著迷信的恐懼向它傾訴，它並不邪惡。它漫不經心隨順自己的習性，我們可以相信它言行一致。

要在宇宙和我們之間有個社會存在，並非不可能。宇宙是我們所有能量和幸福的泉源，看著它如此宏偉又悽然地生長，明白了我們不應該責怪它顯然是無意識的所作所為，我們何不依附它、頌揚它呢？

↗ George Santayana (1863-1952): Reason in Religion
哲學家喬治‧桑塔亞那：《宗教理性》

87　Nature's Ultrahumanity　超越人性的大自然

大自然建立關係是一門科學，也是一門藝術，而不單是知識或感受。我現在更認為，這亦超乎東方的神秘主義、玄學或「冥想方法」等——或者起碼我們西方人在採用冥想方法時，為了讓自己有更正面、更有意義和更有活力的感覺，似乎因而越來越顯得自我耽溺。

我也不認為把大自然變成一種療法，變成崇拜自我感受能力者的免費診所，就能夠企及大自然。

我們疏遠大自然的最微妙難解之因，乃由於我們在某些方面永遠需要去利用大自然，從大自然之中得到私益。我們永遠不會徹底地認識到大自然（或我們自己），當然也永遠不會尊重它，除非我們不再把荒野和「可不可以利用」的觀念聯繫起來（不管那種利用有多麼單純或無害）。我們認為大片的大自然多半是沒用的，這正是我們長久以來之所以敵視和漠視大自然的基礎。

↗ John Fowles (1926-2005): The Tree
英國作家約翰‧福爾斯：《樹木》

88　The Sympathy of Nature　大自然的惻隱之心

那就是大自然的惻隱之心——森林那種野性、未開化的大自然模樣，從未受制於人類法律，也未曾受過高深真理的啟迪……。愛，無論是初生的，或是從死亡般的沈睡中甦醒過來，總會產生一道陽光，讓內心充滿光芒，流溢到外在世界。

↗ Nathaniel Hawthorne (1804-1864): The Scarlet Letter
美國作家霍桑：《紅字》

319

89 Real Enjoyment 真正的享受

對那些可能擁有、且真實有益的享受,人類始終都能獲得,因為人是血肉之軀,一如此刻。特別是在清平時期,我們尤其可能獲得這種享受。看著玉米生長,看著果樹開花結果;喘噓噓地拖著鑊頭或鏟子;看書、思考、戀愛、祈願、禱告——這些都讓人感到幸福……。疲倦的國王或受苦的奴隸,有時也會在庭院地面上的一兩個犁溝裡,找到一個真正屬於自己的王國,擁有一片真正無限的領地。

↗ John Ruskin (1819-1900): Modern Painters
英國作家及藝術評論家約翰·羅斯金:《現代畫家》

90 Experience 經驗

經驗這件事,並非是真的要去汎渡海勒斯海峽,去和托缽僧共舞,或是去投宿廉價客棧。經驗一事乃是關乎感覺和本能,在見聞有意義的事情時,能夠適時留意,並且有所領悟和協調。經驗,並不是指人遇到了些什麼,而是人如何處理所遇到的事情。

↗ Aldous Huxley (1894-1963): Texts and Pretexts
英國作家阿多斯·赫胥黎:《正題與藉口》

91 Thought and Thinking 想法與思考

我們都會沈迷在被稱作「思考」的那種不可思議又愉悦的過程之中,可是一旦要道出我們所思考的東西,哪怕面對面地說,能夠表達出來的卻很少!我們還來不及捕捉,腦海裡的東西便掠過心頭,兀然地消失了,或者它會慢慢沈落,回到一時被閃光所照亮的深暗之處。

↗ Virginia Woolf (1882-1941): The Common Reader
英國女作家吳爾芙:〈一般讀者〉

92 Difference of Opinion 意見分歧

我們很早就學到了這一課:人在表面上儘管有所差異,實際上卻都是一個樣子。我們就是這樣假設我們的夥伴的,所以如果我們發現自己來得早了,發現別人的錶走得比較慢,我們就會失望和生氣。事實上,我們永遠無法互相原諒的唯一過錯,就是意見有所分歧。

↗ Ralph Waldo Emerson (1803-1882): Society and Solitude
美國散文家及詩人愛默生:《社會與孤寂》

93 Conservatives and Radicals 保守派與激進派

在最沒有精力或是最驕奢淫逸的時候,人是保守派。在吃過晚餐尚未就寢之前，在生了病或上了年紀之時，人是保守分子。但是在早上，在智性良心覺醒時，在聽音樂或讀詩時，人又成了激進分子。

↗ Ralph Waldo Emerson (1803-1882): New England Reformers
美國散文家及詩人愛默生：《新英格蘭改革家》

94　Conscience 良心

日積月累的內疚和悔恨，不僅肇因於芝麻小事，也肇因於無傷大雅的樂趣。它們就像垃圾桶，我一生卻都得帶著它們，一想到這裡，我就感到萬物之中就屬人類最無能、最天生不良。

人類擁有七十年的壽命，卻為何只是依然故我，無可救藥地毒害自己的生命？

為何人類把良心當成了死老鼠，扔進井裡，任其腐爛？

↗ Cyril Connolly (1903-1974): The Unquiet Grave
英國作家西裏爾·康諾利：《不平靜的墳墓》

95　Silence 沈默

沈默是天下通行的避難法，是隨所有乏味交談和蠢行之後而來的結果，是撫慰我們各種苦惱的慰藉，無論是厭膩或失望，它都受到歡迎。不論是很傑出還是很拙的畫家，不管前景畫得有多麼糟糕，他都不太會去把背景塗抹掉。背景始終是我們那不可侵犯的避難所，我們在那裡不會受到言行的侮辱或人身的攻擊。

↗ Henry D. Thoreau (1817-1862): A Week on the Concord and Merrimac Rivers
美國作家及思想家亨利·梭羅：《在康科德和梅里馬克河畔度過的一週》

96　Satire 諷刺

諷刺像是某種鏡子，觀者可以從鏡裡認清別人的面目，可是卻看不清自己。這也是諷刺能被世人所接受、鮮少開罪於人的主要原因。就算得罪了人，危險性也不大。長久以來我學到，對於那些我已經使他們理解了諷刺的人，他們的玩笑根本不用去理會：肝火大動雖然可以讓人氣力大增，卻也會讓人心智鬆懈，讓一切心力都泡湯。

↗ Jonathan Swift (1667-1745): The Battle of the Books
喬納森·斯威夫特：《書戲》

97　Idleness 懶散

懶散這種惡習僅限於個人，人可以懶散而不會傷害到別人，也因此它不察地主宰著許多人的生活。懶散看起來並不像會危及財產的詐騙行為，也不像驕傲那樣藉由別人的劣勢來獲取自己的滿足感。懶散具有靜默安詳的特性，不會因為賣弄而惹人嫉妒，也不會因為反對什麼而遭致怨恨，所以沒有人忙於非難或盤查它。

↗ Samuel Johnson (1709-1784): Idleness
英國詩人及評論家塞繆爾·約翰遜：〈懶散〉

98　Hate　仇恨

仇恨之中必有恐懼。仇恨是恐懼的結晶、附贈品和客體化。我們討厭我們所害怕的東西，所以有恨的地方，就潛伏著恐懼。也因此，我們討厭會威脅我們的人身、自由、隱私、收入、聲望、虛榮、夢想或是個人計畫的東西。如果我們能夠在仇恨之中濾出恐懼的因素，或許我們就不會再有仇恨了。

↗ Cyril Connolly (1903-1974): The Unquiet Grave
英國作家西裏爾·康諾利：《不平靜的墳墓》

99　The Beloved　被愛者

「被愛」的人如今有各種樣子。異國異域的人容易刺激戀情的發生，一個年老心智衰退的好爺爺，可能仍愛著二十年前某個午後在齊豪街上所看到的陌生女孩。傳教士可能愛上放蕩女。被愛的這個人可能不忠、油頭粉面、惡習難改，對此，愛他的人可能也和旁人一樣心知肚明，可是卻一點也不會影響愛情的發展。

一個最平凡的人，可能成為美如沼澤毒百合的熾烈愛情的對象；一個好人，可能讓兇暴惡劣的人對其產生愛戀；一個語無倫次的瘋子，可能讓某人的靈魂產生溫柔樸素的田園情調。因此，任何愛情的價值或品質，都是取決於愛者本人。

正因為如此，我們大多數人寧願「愛人」而不是被愛。幾乎人人都想成為愛別人的人。粗略說來，很奇怪的是，很多人竟無法承受被愛的狀態。被愛者有很明白的理由對愛者又怕又恨，因為愛者始終設法想把被愛者看得一清二楚。愛者渴望得到任何與被愛者有關的關係，即使這樣做只會讓自己痛苦。

↗ Carson McCullers (1917-1967): The Ballad of the Sad Café
美國女作家卡森·麥卡勒斯：《傷心咖啡館的民謠》

100　Love　愛情

女士，愛情是個陳舊的字眼，每個人接過它時它是新的，然後耗盡它。它是一個富含意義的字眼，就像一個充滿空氣的囊袋，意義很快就漏掉。它可能會被戳破，就像破了的囊袋一樣，貼了補丁之後又爆炸。而且如果你不擁有它，它也就不會為你存在。人人都談論愛情，但愛情只在擁有愛情的人身上留下痕跡。我並不想多說什麼，因為在所有事情中，就屬談論愛情最為荒謬，而且只有傻子才會去經歷個好幾回。

↗ Ernest Hemingway (1899-1961): Death in the Afternoon
美國作家海明威：《午後死亡》

101　Youth and Lost　青春和失去的青春

在我們年幼時，我們所想像的東西彷彿是實際存在著的（當時尤其有這種感覺）。我們處在沈睡與清醒之間，能瞥見模糊但美好的奇形怪狀之物，而且總會出現比真實所見更加美好的東西。

在夢裡，充足的血液讓腦際所幻想出的東西變得溫暖且真實，在我們年輕時，我們的思緒如此地被蓬勃的朝氣所滋養呵護。我們無牽無掛快樂地呼吸著，未來的重任催促著有力的心跳，我們把不可動搖的信心寄託於真與善。

隨著年事增長，我們把累積下來的歡樂和希望都給耗盡。我們不再裹在羔羊的羊毛裡，不再在樂園裡被哄睡。在我們品嚐生活的樂趣之時，樂趣的精神卻消失，感覺變得疲乏，只留下一些空洞不實、沒有生氣的過往雲煙之物！

↗ William Hazlitt (1778-1830): My First Acquaintance With Poets
英國隨筆作家威廉‧哈茲裏特：《初識詩人》

102　Age　年歲

年紀愈大，時間就愈感覺短促……。年輕時，我們在每天的每個時刻裡，都可能有全新的主觀或客觀經驗。那時領悟力佳，記憶力好，那段時期的回憶就像一場快腳步的有趣旅遊，內容雜亂而豐富，時間也被拉長。但隨著歲月一年一年地過去，這種經驗變成一種無意識的例行生活，我們一點也不再留心。時間一天天一週週地流逝，沒有在記憶裡留下些什麼，一年也就比一年變得更加空洞虛擲。

↗ William James (1842-1910): Principles of Psychology
美國哲學家及心理學家威廉‧詹姆斯：《心理學原理》

103　How to Grow Old　如何安度晚年

年老的時候，在心理上要避免兩種危險。第一，不要過分沈緬於過去。活在回憶之中，為過去而抱憾，為逝去的友人而哀傷，這對生活無濟於事。人應該往前看，看那些仍可以有所作為的事情。

但這並不容易，因為個人的過去會慢慢變得愈加沉重。人們很容易以為，以前的情感比現在更加生動，以前的心智比現在更加敏銳。如果以上所説的是真的，那就應該把回憶忘掉；如果回憶能被忘掉，那它就不再是真的了。

第二件要避免的事情，就是執著於青春，打著想取得年輕活力的主意。小孩子大了，有自己的生活要過，如果你仍像他們小時候那樣對他們關心備至，那你就很可能成為他們的負擔，除非他們太過於麻木。我的意思並不是說要對他們不聞不問，而是給的關心要理性，如果可能，也要博愛，而不要過度的情緒化。

↗ Bertrand Russell (1872-1970) 英國哲學家羅素

104　A Spring Without Voices　寂靜的春天

隨後一種奇怪的枯萎病在這個地方蔓延開來，一切開始變化。這個社區被下了魔咒：莫名其妙的疾病席捲雞群，牛羊也病亡。到處都籠罩著死亡的陰影。農夫們談論著家人得了重病，病人出現的新型病症，讓城裡的大夫愈來愈糊塗。

有幾樁病因不明的猝死，不只發生在成人身上，也發生在兒童身上。兒童們在玩耍時突然染上病，幾小時之內便死去。

這一片寂靜顯得詭異。譬如說，鳥兒都到哪裡去了？許多人困惑不安地在談論著。後院的餵養台都荒廢了，到處可見幾隻小鳥在垂死掙扎，牠們劇烈地顫抖，再也飛不起來。這是一個無聲的春天，知更鳥、貓鵲、野鴿、松鴉、鷦鷯和其他鳥在清晨時的黎明大合唱，已不復聞，只有一片寂靜籠罩著田野、樹林和沼澤。

↗ Rachel Carson (1907-1964): Silent Spring
美國生物學家、環境學家及作家瑞秋‧卡森：《寂靜的春天》

105　The Dog　狗

這個人救了牠的命，這很難得，但更難能可貴的是，他是個完美的主人。別人對狗好是出於責任感或事業上的利益，他對狗好，是天性使然，他把狗當成孩子。再者，他從不會忘記親切地跟狗打招呼，或是說句鼓勵的話，然後坐下來和牠們長聊（他說，他們這樣做是在閒扯），這讓他覺得很開心，狗兒們也很興奮。

↗ Jack London (1876-1916): The Call of the Wild
美國作家傑克‧倫敦：《野性的呼喚》

106　Childhood　童年

我小時候的記憶比許多人模糊：不知道為什麼，童年一結束，我就別過臉去，但我知道決不是因為有著痛苦回憶這種常見的原因。

關於這一點，多年來一直困擾著我，但後來我發現，兒時舊事，通常不足以採信。有些人搬出好些昔日的盛事趣事來聊以自慰，有些人則念念不忘或真實或想像而來的痛苦，把它當成自己何以變得如此的口實。

我想我一向清楚自己的記性，知道哪一段時間的記憶足以採信，明白生活中在何時又摻進了夢想或幻想。做過的夢和對夢想的需要，扭曲了發生的事件。我也很早就瞭解到，獨生子之所以大吵大鬧，是做惡夢之後所扭曲的結果。然而，對於茱麗亞的回憶，我百分之百相信是確實無誤的。

↗ Lillian Hellman (1905-1984): Julia
美國女劇作家莉莉安‧海爾曼：《茱麗亞》

107 Writers 作家

他是個三十五歲的男人，看上去卻像五十歲。他童山濯濯，有靜脈曲張，戴著眼鏡，或者說，如果他唯一的那副眼鏡沒有丟掉太久的話，那他就會戴上眼鏡。情況正常時，他會營養不良，而如果他近來交了一陣好運，那他就會有宿醉之苦。

現在已經是上午十一點半，按照時間表，他兩個鐘頭前就應該開始工作了。不過即使他認真地想開始工作，卻百般受阻，像是電話鈴聲響個不停，嬰兒叫喊，外面街上的電鑽聲噠噠噠的，還有債主走上樓的沈重皮靴聲。最後一次的打斷是第二班郵件的到來，捎來了兩份傳單和一份印著赤字的所得稅催繳單。

不用說，這號人物就是位作家。

↗ George Orwell (1903-1950): Confessions of a Book Reviewer
英國小說家及散文家喬治‧奧威爾：《一位書評家的自白》

108 Happy Life 幸福的人生

離開桑菲德我很難過：我愛桑菲德。我愛這個地方，因為我在這裡過了一段充實快樂的生活，最起碼我有過這麼一小段時光。

沒有人欺負過我，我也沒有受到過驚嚇，沒有湮沒在僕人之中，讓他們把契合於燦爛、活力和快感的光芒都給驅逐了。我已經面對面地和我所敬愛的人談過話了——那是一個有獨創性、有活力，而且心胸開闊的人。我已經認識了你，羅徹斯特先生，當我感到自己勢必與你永別，我就又害怕又痛苦。我看到自己不得不離去，這就好像我知道人必定一死一樣。

↗ Charlotte Bronte (1816-1855): Jane Eyre
英國女作家夏洛蒂‧勃朗特：《簡‧愛》

109 Day 白晝

黛絲目前的唯一活動是在天黑之後；當她走進森林裡，她似乎才會最沒有孤獨感。她知道怎麼抓住黃昏的片刻：那時，明暗平分天色，白天裡的壓抑與夜晚的牽掛相互抵銷，留下絕對的心靈自由，活著的苦痛爾後降至最低。

她並不害怕陰暗，她僅有的念頭似乎就是想規避人群，或者說，世界這個冰冷的生長物，整體看來很駭人，可是它的個體非但不足為懼，甚至還很可憐。

↗ Thomas Hardy (1840-1928): Tess of the D'Urbervilles
英國小說家及詩人托馬斯‧哈代：《黛絲姑娘》

110　The Rabbits and the Wolves　兔子與狼

在年幼孩童的記憶中，有一窩兔子住在狼群附近。狼群聲稱牠們不喜歡兔子的生活方式。（狼群很著迷自己的生活方式，因為那是牠們唯一的生活方式。）

一天夜裡，幾隻狼死於一場地震，於是把這件事怪罪於兔子，因為大家都知道兔子用後腿蹬地面，因此發生了地震。又一天夜裡，有一隻狼死於一道閃電，兔子又被怪罪，因為大家知道吃萵苣者會引來閃電。

狼群威脅兔子如果不規矩點，就要好好教化教化牠們，兔子因此決定逃往荒島。可是其他住在遠處的動物羞辱兔子說：「你們應該待在原處，要勇敢些，這個世界容不得逃避現實。要是狼群攻擊你們，我們很可能會來助你們一臂之力。」

於是兔子繼續住在狼群附近。有一天，洪水大作，淹死很多狼，兔子還是被怪罪，因為大家都知道長耳朵的吃胡蘿蔔者引來了洪水。狼群於是為了自己的利益，便突襲兔子，為求自我保護，便把兔子關進了黑暗的山洞裡。

幾個星期以來都沒有兔子們的消息，其他的動物想知道牠們發生了什麼事。狼群表示，兔子已經被吃掉，而既然牠們已經被吃掉，這件事情就成了單純的內部問題。

其他動物警告狼群說，除非狼群能夠說出吃掉兔子的理由，否則大夥就有可能要聯合起來對付牠們，於是牠們便給了一個原因。

狼群說：「因為牠們想逃避。你們都知道，這個世界是容不下逃避現實的人的。」

↗ James Thurber (1894-1961): The Rabbits Who Caused All the Trouble
美國作家詹姆士‧瑟伯：《招惹麻煩的兔子》

111　The Depths of Heart　內心深處

在每個人的內心深處，都有一座墳墓和土牢，上面的燈光、音樂和喧囂狂歡，或許可以讓我們把它們忘掉，把墓中死者和牢中匿身的犯人都忘記。但有時候，多半在深夜裡，那些黑暗之處會猛然敞開。

在這樣的時刻裡，內心沒有自主的力量，只能消極地感受；想像力栩栩如生地寫照出所有的想法，卻無法加以選擇或控制；於是你祈禱你能夠停止憂愁，祈禱和憂愁相伴的懊悔不會掙脫而出。

↗ Nathaniel Hawthorne (1804-1864): The Haunted Mind
美國作家霍桑：《神魂不安》

112　The Moon　月亮

　　月亮是一片白色的奇異天地，它又大又白，像個柔軟的球，掛在夜空上。它穿越太空到底想傳遞什麼給我，我永遠也弄不清楚。月亮牽引潮汐，調節婦女的經期，觸動瘋子，它不只是天文學家眼中死寂的一團東西。……我們形容月亮死氣沈沈，其實是在說我們自己死氣沈沈。我們發現太空如此虛空可怕，其實是在描繪我們自己那種難忍的空虛。

　　↗ D. H. Lawrence (1885-1930): Introduction to The Dragon of the Apocalypse by
　　　Frederick Carter 英國作家勞倫斯：《弗德雷克·卡特啟示篇的魔力》之引論

113　Birth　誕生

誕生猶如入睡與遺忘；
伴同我們昇起的靈魂，
這遠方來的生命之星，
已經沈落在別的地方；
不是在全然的遺忘中，

不是在全然的裸露中，
而是在蔓生的雲輝裡
我們來自上帝這家鄉：
繦褓時天堂就在身旁！

　　　　↗ William Wordsworth (1770-1850): Ode: Intimations of Immortality
　　　　　英國詩人威廉·華茲華斯：《不朽的徵兆》

114　My Heart Leaps Up　我怦然心動

凝視天邊的彩虹
會讓我怦然心動；
我生命之初如此；
而今成人仍如此；
我老了亦當如此，

否則我寧可死去！
赤子是成人之父；
願天生的虔敬心
相繫我的一天天。

　　　　　　↗ William Wordsworth (1770-1850)
　　　　　　　英國詩人威廉·華茲華斯

115　Joy and Sorrow　喜悅與悲傷

你生命的悲傷刻畫得愈深，
所能容納的喜悅就愈多。
盛著你的酒的那支杯子，
不正是陶匠爐中所燒烤過的那支嗎？
撫慰你的心靈的那把琴，
不正是被刀刨空了的木頭嗎？
當你充滿喜悅時，觀照你的心靈深處，
你會發現，讓你悲傷的事，

正是那讓你喜悅的事。
又當你悲傷時，再看看自己的內心，
你會明白，你所哭泣的事，
正是那曾經令你快樂的事。
有人說：「喜悅比悲傷崇高。」
有人說：「不，悲傷比較崇高。」
而我說，它們是形影不離的。
……
你就像秤錘懸在
喜悅與悲傷之間。
惟有你空無一念時，
才能靜止平衡。

↗ Kahlil Gibran (1883-1931): The Prophet
黎巴嫩裔美國詩人紀伯侖：《先知》

116　Freedom　自由

你終會自由，
但不是當日子無牽無掛時，
或是夜裡不再匱乏悲傷時，
而是當事情困擾著生活時，
你能無拘無束地跳脫出來。
……
事實上你所謂的自由，
才是最大的枷鎖，
儘管枷鎖在陽光下會閃閃發光，令
　　人眩目。

你為了自由而想拋棄的東西，
不正是你自己的一部分嗎？
……
你想擺脫的牽掛，
是你自取的，
並沒有人強加給你。
你想驅散的恐懼，
存在你心中，
而不是被放在你手上。

↗ Kahlil Gibran (1883-1931): The Prophet
黎巴嫩裔美國詩人紀伯侖：《先知》

117　Let Me Enjoy the Earth No Less　讓我盡情享受塵世之樂

讓我盡情享受塵世之樂，
因為那制定萬物的力量
所創造出的人世間美好
並非以我的歡樂為目的。

我身旁擦掠過一位佳人，

在動人詩歌的手抄本中，
未知的場景和夢賜靈感，
我傾瀉他人的狂喜之情
就好像是我自己的狂喜。

此後有朝一日走向天堂

沒向我説話未對我示意；
我讚美不屬於我的雙唇，
陶醉在她冷漠的神情裡。

和天堂居民——若真有其事——
我會很高興地抬眼遙望，
儘管那裡並沒我的位置。

↗ Thomas Hardy (1840-1928)
英國小說家及詩人托馬斯·哈代

118　Work　工作

你也曾聽説，生命是黑暗的，
你疲勞之時便附和那些疲勞的人所説的話。
我説生命的確是黑暗的，除非懷有熱切的渴望，
但所有的熱切渴望都是盲目的，除非具有知識；
所有的知識都是徒然的，除非付諸行動工作；
所有的工作都是徒勞的，除非擁有愛；
當你懷著愛心工作，你便是把自己、他人和神
相繫在一塊兒。

工作是愛的體現。
如果你無法懷著愛工作，卻只是滿心怨恨，
那就最好放下工作，
坐在寺廟門前，
接受樂在工作的人的接濟吧。
因為你烘焙麵包時若漫不經心，
那你烤出來的麵包就會是苦的，
只能讓人勉強裏腹。
如果你榨葡萄時心不甘情不願，
你的怨氣就會變成毒汁，滲入酒中。
如果你歌聲如天使，
卻不愛歌唱，
那你就把人們的耳朵搗起來吧，
讓白天或夜裡的聲音他們都聽不到。

↗ Kahlil Gibran (1883-1931): The Prophet
黎巴嫩裔美國詩人紀伯侖：《先知》

119　The Road Not Taken　沒有走的路

黃色森林岔出兩條路，

黎明時路都蓋滿落葉，

329

可惜我不能兩條都走。　　　　　尚沒有人跡踏足其上，
我這個旅人佇立良久，　　　　　前一條路改天再走吧！
極目遠眺其中一條路，　　　　　我知路如何分歧而去，
看著它轉進灌木林裡。　　　　　也懷疑自己能夠返回……

我選別條同樣美的路，　　　　　多年多年之後在某地，
這條路長滿草少行跡，　　　　　我會嘆口氣講這件事：
選它似乎較有些道理；　　　　　樹林子裡岔出兩條路，而我呢——
雖實際上的來來往往，　　　　　我選了人跡少的那條，
已經使它們相差無幾。　　　　　千差萬別就由此而起。

↗ Robert Frost (1874-1963) 美國詩人羅伯特‧弗斯特

120　Our Bias 我們的偏見

沙漏對著獅爪低語，　　　　　或動搖玫瑰的自信。
鐘樓日夜傾訴花園，　　　　　因它們只想著成功；
時間容忍多少錯誤，　　　　　我們憑字音選字辭，
說它永無誤多謬誤。　　　　　看粗劣來判斷問題；
　　　　　　　　　　　　　　我們愛與時間相伴。
不管沙漏流得多快，　　　　　我們不都愛兜圈子
鐘聲多麼洪亮深沈，　　　　　而非直達現況的嗎？
時間不能阻擋獅躍，

↗ Wystan Hush Auden (1907-1973)
英國詩人、劇作家及批評家奧登

121　What It Is To Love 戀愛是怎麼一回事

好心的牧人，告訴這小夥子戀愛是怎麼一回事。
戀愛就是嘆息與流淚；
……
就是忠心耿耿，終日效勞；
……
就是幻想，
就是一腔激情，滿心殷盼；
就是傾心仰慕，承擔義務，唯命是從，
畢恭畢敬，充滿耐性又坐立難安，
一派純潔，一切考驗，一切順從。

↗ William Shakespeare (1564-1616): As You Like It (Act 5 Scene 2)
英國大文豪威廉·莎士比亞:《皆大歡喜》5 幕 2 場

122　When You Are Old　當你老了

當你年老髮白睡意濃,
爐旁打盹拿起這書時,
慢慢翻讀回想你眼裡
曾有過的柔和與濃愁;

多少人愛你的恬逸樣,
假意真心戀著你的美,

卻有人愛你的朝聖者靈魂,
愛你色衰之後的愁容;

在紅光爐旁低下腰來,
淒然呢喃愛情的消逝,
在上頭的山上踱方步,
把他的臉藏在群星中。

↗ William Butler Yeats (1865-1939)
愛爾蘭詩人葉慈

國家圖書館出版品預行編目資料

愛‧英閱：擁抱英語文選／深度閱讀合輯
/ Michaeline Wu & Bai Yang 著--初版.
–[臺北市] 寂天文化, 2017.05 面 ;公分. --

ISBN：978-986-184-813-6（25K 平裝附光碟片）
ISBN：978-986-184-977-5（25K 精裝附光碟片）
ISBN：978-986-184-574-1（20K 平裝附光碟片）

1. 英語　　2. 讀本

805.18　　　　　　　　　　　106005953

作者	Michaeline Wu / Bai Yang
審定者	Dennis Le Boeuf & Liming Jing
編輯	李盈瑩
主編	黃鈺云
製程管理	洪巧玲
出版者	寂天文化事業股份有限公司
電話	02-2365-9739
傳真	02-2365-9835
網址	www.icosmos.com.tw
讀者服務	onlineservice@icosmos.com.tw

本書為《擁抱英語文選》與《深度閱讀：英語文選集》之合輯
Copyright©2010 by Cosmos Culture Ltd.
版權所有　請勿翻印
出版日期 2017 年 5 月初版三刷　　　200101

郵撥帳號 1998620-0（寂天文化事業股份有限公司）
▪ 劃撥金額 600（含）元以上者，郵資免費。
▪ 訂購金額 600 元以下者，請外加 65 元。
【若有破損，請寄回更換，謝謝。】